The Peterborough Project

A CASE STUDY OF EDUCATIONAL CHANGE AND INNOVATION

H.H. Russell, K.A. Leithwood, R.P. Baxter

Research in Education Series No. 2
The Ontario Institute for Studies in Education

THE ONTARIO INSTITUTE FOR STUDIES IN EDUCATION
has three prime functions: to conduct programs of graduate study in education, to undertake research in education, and to assist in the implementation of the findings of educational studies. The Institute is a college chartered by an Act of the Ontario Legislature in 1965. It is affiliated with the University of Toronto for graduate studies purposes.

© The Ontario Institute for Studies in Education 1973
252 Bloor Street West, Toronto M5S 1V6

ISBN 0-7744-0089-7   Printed in Canada

Contents

CHAPTER 1 **Introduction/1**
Background to the Project/1
Rationale for the Project/3
Purpose of the Study/5

2 **Some important studies of diffusion/7**
Research Traditions/7
Adoption Models/8
Diffusion Models/8
Diffusion Research Variables and Hypotheses/9
Some Basic Problems/13

3 **Application of diffusion literature/15**
The Adoption Process/15
Diffusion Variables/17
Cost Variables/17
Compatibility/18
Complexity/20
Other Variables/20

4 **The diffusion process/23**
Establishing the Study Group (Goal identification; Schools, problems, and solutions; Study group innovations; Implementation of innovations)/25
A Modified Plan for Diffusion/32
Communication Network/36
Characteristics of Innovations under Consideration/38
Outside the Project County/39
Conclusion/40

5 **Development of innovative programs/41**
Local Curriculum Development/42
Educational Objectives/43
Project Curricula and Schools (School A; School B; School C; School D; School E)/46

Individually Prescribed Instruction (Mathematics)/51
Conceptual Skills Program/53
OTF Science Program/53
Other Common Components/54

CHAPTER 6 **The role of evaluation in school change: theoretical considerations/55**
Goal of Evaluation/55
Functions of Evaluation/56
Utility and Feasibility of Operational Objectives/57
Theoretical Shortcomings of Student Performance Objectives/59
Problems in Operationalizing Student Performance Objectives/60
The Design of Educational Evaluation (The choice of design; Evaluating student achievement – Criterion-referenced measurement; Multiple-matrix sampling)/66
The Project Evaluation Model/75

7 **Evaluation of some project components/78**
School C Mathematics (Method; Results)/80
School A Social Studies (Method; Results)/82
Conceptual Skills Program (Method; Results)/83
Individually Prescribed Instruction: Mathematics (Method; Results)/87

8 **Toward a model for educational change and innovation/104**
Academic–School Interaction/104
Climate for Change/106
Roles of Evaluation/106
Curriculum Development Strategies/107
Interschool Cooperation and County-wide Communication Network/107
Teacher Responsibility for Change/108
Relationship of the Model's Components (Stage 1: Agreements to begin; Stage 2: Establish organization; Stage 3: Problem and goal selection; Stage 4: Study available solutions; Stage 5: Pilot trial; Stage 6: Adopt, adapt, or reject; Stage 7: Field trial)/108
Conclusion/114

Appendix/117

References/135

FIGURES
1. Stages in the development of a workable structure for process and product diffusion among schools in the Project/34
2. Implementation communication network/36
3. A strategy used by teachers in developing curriculum/43
4. CEMREL evaluation model/76
5. Components of the evaluation of the Project/77
6. Information provided by a pretest–posttest experimental design when repeated over two or more years/79
7. School change model: interaction of components/112
8. Change model as a matrix suggesting potential areas for hypothesis testing/114

TABLES (Appendix)
1. School C Math, Grades 4–6, 1970/71: Means and Standard Deviations/118
2. School C Math, Grade 4, 1970/71: Means and Standard Deviations, by Skill Area/119
3. School C Math, Grade 5, 1970/71: Means and Standard Deviations, by Skill Area/120
4. School C Math, Grade 6, 1970/71: Means and Standard Deviations, by Skill Area/122
5. School C Math, Grade 4, 1970/71: Correlations on Main Variables/123
6. School A Social Studies, Grades 4–6, 1970/71: Means and Standard Deviations on Main Variables/124
7. Conceptual Skills, 1970/71: Case Study Group Means and Standard Deviations on Main Variables, by SES Level/125
8. Conceptual Skills, 1970/71: Analysis of Variance of CRM Posttest Scores/125
9. Conceptual Skills, 1970/71: Case Study Group Means on CRM Posttest Scores/125
10. Conceptual Skills, 1970/71: Correlations for Case Study Groups Using Within-group Data/126
11. Conceptual Skills, 1970/71: Means and Standard Deviations on Main Variables/127
12. IPI Mathematics, Grades 4–6, 1970/71: Means and Standard Deviations on Main Variables/128
13. IPI Mathematics, Grades 4–6, 1970/71: Correlations, All Subjects/130
14. IPI Mathematics: Number of Students in Project Schools in the IPI Curriculum at End of the 1970/71 School Year, by Level/131
15. IPI Mathematics: Number of Students in Alberta Schools in the IPI Curriculum at End of the 1969/70 School Year, by Level/131
16. IPI Mathematics: Number of Students in Oakleaf School in the IPI Curriculum at End of the 1967/68 School Year, by Level/132
17. IPI Mathematics: Percentage of Grade 5 Pupils Involved in Major Categories of Classroom Activities in an IPI School/132
18. IPI Mathematics, 1970/71: Percentage of Pupil Time Observed in Prespecified Activities/133

CHAPTER 1

Introduction

BACKGROUND TO THE PROJECT The Peterborough Project is an ongoing project of educational innovation. It was initiated early in 1969 by a number of elementary school principals in Peterborough County, Ontario, in cooperation with the Ontario Institute for Studies in Education (OISE). In its early stages – known as Phase I (POISE) – the Project dealt with problems identified at the school level, largely by cooperating groups of classroom teachers within each school.[1] In September 1969, OISE's field center, the Trent Valley Centre (TVC), was established in Peterborough to serve the Ministry of Education's Region 9. The TVC is part of the Ontario Institute for Studies in Education and the Department of Educational Theory of the University of Toronto; as such, its primary business is educational theory, broadly conceived. The establishment of the TVC corresponded closely with a gradual but significant change in focus in the Project.

At the time the TVC was established, the programming problem for the Centre was defined generally as the identification of a vehicle for channeling the felt needs of the schools in the region to the academics within OISE and channeling OISE manpower and research knowledge to schools in regions that were involved in change. Such a vehicle required the following characteristics:

1. It should deal with problems identified at the school level, as opposed to the academic level (that is, those concerning students, teachers, principals, directors, departmental consultants, and others engaged directly in the schools).

2. It should employ the services of qualified academics for the solution of problems that are amenable to academic intervention (such as measurement and evaluation,

---

[1]Phase 1 has been thoroughly described in Benson et al. (1969).

computer systems, administration models, curriculum theory, curriculum materials, psychology, sociology, planning, history, and philosophy).

3. It should have the potential for yielding general solutions as opposed to school-specific solutions.

4. It should utilize the expertise of non-OISE and nonschool personnel (such as departmental consultants and staff members from regional universities, teachers' colleges, and other institutions).

5. It should encourage the academic manpower development of the region's teachers, principals, and high-level staff through graduate instruction and thesis work.

6. It should provide for the development of all varieties of manpower within the region with a view to phased withdrawal of OISE manpower.

By September 1969, Phase 1 of the Project had already acquired a number of the features described above, and it was clear that those features that were missing could be readily incorporated. It was natural, then, for the TVC to adopt the Project as a vehicle for its initial work. At the same time, the Project could employ the TVC as a legitimate alternate for OISE input.

The original components of the Project that were planned prior to the establishment of the TVC remained essentially unchanged by this reciprocal arrangement.[2] In fact, many of the Project's process considerations were incorporated as primary ingredients of the TVC program. The TVC did influence the Project, however, by shifting its focus. Instead of concentrating on school-specific improvement of education within participating schools, it began to emphasize the generalizability of the conclusions that could be made pertaining to the effects of specific innovations. This new concern – labeled here as Phase 2 – required a careful description of all features of the original program components and their later adaptations, as well as a careful assessment of student performance through each of the phases of program development.

In Phase 1, five schools were involved in the Project's program of educational innovation. These comprised the Core Group. In Phase 2, activities were extended to another twelve schools, which constituted the Study Group. By the summer of 1972, when Phase 3 was under way, all forty-eight schools in Peterborough County were involved in major change activities. These stemmed in large part from the activities described in this book (with important modifications and new developments discussed elsewhere[3]).

---

[2]The major components of the present study are described in chapter 5.
[3]The mathematics workshop series: Interim progress report. A joint paper of the Peterborough Board of Education and the Trent Valley Centre, 1972.

RATIONALE FOR THE PROJECT

Typically, innovations are introduced to facilitate the achievement of existing school goals or objectives. They also may be designed to achieve new and more desirable goals, or to increase the proportion of students who achieve objectives. Whatever the underlying purpose, evaluation is essential to any program of innovation to measure the exact benefit that results from its implementation and to determine whether or not its cost is prohibitive.[4]

In the event that any gains can be or are made through innovation in a school setting, extension of the benefits to a wider range of people is warranted. This may be achieved either by dissemination or by diffusion. It is important that these be recognized as two distinct alternative processes. Dissemination involves the communication of an innovative idea by a central or knowledgeable agent to a representative or representatives of a social system at a specific point in time. Diffusion begins with dissemination and also involves the communication of the idea by the representatives of the system to their peers or to other individuals for whom the innovation has been designed. The Peterborough Project emphasizes not only the description of the diffusion process and the rate of diffusion, but also the construction of a social system designed to foster diffusion. It stresses evaluation of the social system at the formative level, so that changes in the system can be effected in such a way as to improve the diffusion process in practice. Thus, the Project favors planned diffusion as being potentially more effective than unplanned diffusion or standard dissemination activities.

The reasons for innovating, evaluating, and planning the diffusion of innovations in education may seem self-evident. But there are two very basic questions that must be considered before any program of educational innovation is implemented: first, who selects educational objectives; and second, who decides which innovations will be adopted or rejected?

When the focus is on national objectives, educational goals are set by publicly elected representatives of the people, and these are the persons to whom educators are accountable. In the past, the implicit goals established by our national leaders have been to increase the amount of time that each student spends in school, to increase the number of students benefiting from school, and to increase the proportion of students attaining graduation status in the higher levels of education. These variables have been related, with some success, to the gross national product (Denison, 1964, p. 23); and GNP has therefore been regarded – particularly by economists – as a convenient indicator of educational attainment.

---

[4]In some instances, it may be possible to reduce the dollar or manpower costs, and here even a zero gain may be a worthwhile result.

It has been suggested that GNP is an inadequate measure of improvement within a society (Galbraith, 1958, p. 124), and we feel that this is particularly true in the case of education. Economists in education and educational administrators should accommodate their views to the position taken by Denison (1962): "[GNP] can deal only with changes in the amount of formal education received by members of the labour force, it cannot take into account changes (presumably improvements) in the quality of the day's schooling [p. 67]." Denison also raises the question of whether schools can teach as much in less time or at less cost through attention to the critical objectives being achieved, and through innovative means maximize student attainment of the objectives. We have been influenced by such considerations, and our attention to precise assessment of student performance on educational objectives is an essential ingredient in the Project and the central thrust of this case study report.

When national leaders are responsible for setting educational goals, either explicitly or implicitly, it seems that the accountability issue is relatively clear and that attention to specific student performance objectives will probably lead educational researchers and educational administrators in the right direction. Unique problems arise, however, in setting educational goals for a large unit of jurisdiction, whether supranational, national, or subnational. Even the act of goal setting may be dysfunctional. Dewey (1966) has commented as follows on the effects of nationally or externally imposed goals:

> The vice of externally imposed ends has deep roots. Teachers receive them from superior authorities; these authorities accept them from what is current in the community. The teachers impose them on children. As a first consequence, the intelligence of the teacher is not free; it is confined to receiving the aims laid down from above. Too rarely is the individual teacher so free from the dictation of authoritative supervisor, textbook on methods, prescribed course of study, etc., that he can let his mind come to close quarters with the pupil's mind and the subject matter. This distrust of the teacher's experience is then reflected in lack of confidence in the responses of pupils. The latter receive their aims through a double or treble external imposition, and are constantly confused by the conflict between the aims which are natural to their own experience at the time and those in which they are taught to acquiesce. Until the democratic criterion of the intrinsic significance of every growing experience is recognized, we shall be intellectually confused by the demand for adaptation to external aims. [P. 8]

The Peterborough Project has recognized the basic significance of this comment and accepts some responsibility for influencing educators in considering aims of education that are rooted in the students and the people of the school community. The acceptance of such a view does not necessarily exclude the possibility of educational objectives for large jurisdictional units; in fact, the need for such aims is obvious. But they must be sufficiently general that individual students and teachers will be free to identify and pursue specific local and individual goals.

A. N. Whitehead (1956) provides even more precise guidelines for the identification of the person or persons who should have responsibility for specifying educational objectives: "The first requisite for educational reform is the school as a unit with its approved curriculum based on its own needs and evolved by its own staff [p. 21]."

If the advice of Dewey and Whitehead is sound, as it appears to be, the answers to the two questions raised earlier must accommodate and reflect a high degree of school autonomy and individual freedom.

Independently of the issue of compatibility between school goals and national goals, there is good reason to study school goals carefully, and to assess accurately the attainment of them and their specific subgoals or of student performance objectives. The student performance data acquired through evaluation can serve as a reasonable starting point for the consideration of school change and the introduction of innovation.

The identification of innovative programs that are compatible with student needs and the community's ability to pay the cost is a sophisticated business that sometimes leads to the adoption of rigidly packaged programs. It may lead also to the preparation of programs designed within and specifically for a particular school. Whatever the innovation, the adoption–rejection decision must be related to precise evaluation data; and in cases where positive benefits are the clear result of an innovative program, the implementation of an effective diffusion program can magnify and multiply the benefits for a larger population of students.

PURPOSE OF THE STUDY

Our purpose in describing and analyzing the Peterborough Project is threefold. First, we wish to demonstrate that educational theory and practice can be successfully and productively fused in a school setting. There are several ways of doing this, the most obvious being the application of accepted theoretical principles to the practical problems arising in the design and conduct of the Project.

Second, we hope to outline a significant role for rigorous scientific methodology in the improvement of educational practice. One methodological feature of the Project that distinguishes it from many other studies of its type is its elaborate evaluation procedure. This process involves student performance objectives and criterion-referenced testing, pilot trial and field testing, experimental design considerations, and hypothesis testing, and thus is related to the more basic processes of change and diffusion.

Third, and most important, we wish to suggest that the problems of educational change are highly complex and that linear strategies of educational development followed by characteristic attempts at installing those products of development in schools can and should be vastly improved upon. We have therefore conceptualized a working model for school change that depends on a high degree of school autonomy in curriculum decisions, as well as on classroom teachers' acceptance of central responsibility for the school curriculum.

CHAPTER 2

Some important studies of diffusion

RESEARCH TRADITIONS

The Peterborough Project and the related program of the Trent Valley Centre may possess some novel features or novel combinations of well-known features of diffusion activities, but they do not constitute a novel discipline or a novel class of studies. Diffusion has been a subject for research in at least six disciplines or study areas. Although cross-fertilization among these disciplines is a relatively recent development, it is worth reviewing some landmark studies that may have bearing on what has happened, will happen, or should happen in connection with the Project.

Diffusion studies in anthropology are concerned with participant observation methods for data collection and focus on the social consequences of innovations. Such studies provide a rich background for careful interpretation of observational data (Rogers, 1962, p. 25). In sociology, the pioneering work of Tarde in 1903 focuses attention on the adoption of innovations over time (Rogers, 1962, p. 28). His early work has given direction to a number of subsequent studies. Rural sociology also has a strong tradition in the study of diffusion, and its particular array of studies is concerned mainly with the role of various agents and development groups in the introduction of agricultural innovations.

The tradition in education dates back to the early research by Mort on school finance in the 1920s (Rogers, 1962). There was a subsequent lapse of interest until the 1950s, but since then many more studies have been produced. More recent research on diffusion has originated in the areas of industrial communication and medicine.

Although an impressive number of studies have been undertaken in all these disciplines, no comprehensive and generally accepted theory of diffusion has emerged in the literature. Rogers (1962, pp. 308–11) identifies the need for such a theory and proposes a number of ground rules on which to base it. He also provides some tentative models of various processes related to diffusion. We shall examine one of these – his model of the adoption process – and a similar model developed by Watson (1967).

ADOPTION MODELS In describing the adoption process, Rogers (1962, ch. 4) identifies five consecutive stages that are followed in all learning: awareness, interest, evaluation, trial, and adoption. Since the word *evaluation* has a rather special technical meaning in education literature, it is important to note that Rogers uses it to refer to mental activity that involves the weighing of advantages and disadvantages of the proposed change. No physical weighing takes place, nor is there any gathering of empirical data.

Watson (1967, pp. 106–15) has constructed a model similar to Rogers's, dealing with the concept of self-renewal within the school system. He identifies ten stages that are essentially parallel to Rogers's five: sensing, screening, diagnosing, inventing, weighing, deciding, introducing, operating, evaluating, and revising. The sensing and awareness stages are clearly substitutable; screening, diagnosing, and inventing probably are comparable to Rogers's interest stage. The operating, evaluating, and revising stages correspond generally to Rogers's trial stage. Watson uses the term *evaluating* to refer to what Scriven (1967) has called formative evaluation, whereby preliminary trials are conducted for the purpose of adopting or revising the draft innovation.

Other models have been developed that are related to the adoption process and indicate rates of adoption or acceptance of innovation. Some of these distribution models will be discussed later in connection with the Peterborough Project.

DIFFUSION MODELS Diffusion models are distinct from adoption models in that they apply to a broader context. For example, a study of diffusion conducted by a more or less typical school or school community can be considered representative of a larger population of schools or communities, and observations about a particular model may be generalized to the point where predictions about comparable schools and school systems may be tentatively proposed.

In one important publication (the Committee on the Implementation of Change, 1967), the case study of Ryerson Heights Elementary School is described in detail and may be considered a working model of an individual school. The many steps involve planned change over the basic stages identified by Rogers and Watson, and include many adaptations to permit accommodation to a local setting. Another case study described in the same book is the Boston Strategy, introduced within the

Cooperative Project for Educational Development (COPED). This program is designed to train action researchers in the classrooms. The team members, or teachers, are the internal change agents, and they work with external agents through seminars or clinics at an affiliated university. The team members are released from about a quarter of their teaching duties to perform this task. A second model or strategy described under the COPED label involves the school principal, school psychologists, and elementary guidance counselors. In this case, the first step is to build a group of interested intermediaries who eventually will consult teachers or groups of teachers. Here the stages are identified as classroom diagnosis, innovation, feedback, and evaluation.

Another project, SUCCEED, has been described and implemented by Hummell and Cox (1970). In this case, the external agents consist of four academics from the Learning Research and Development Center of Pittsburgh, and the internal agents are regular classroom teachers. The latter are granted released time for the intensive training sessions that are designed to make them the critical change agents. The emphasis in the SUCCEED program is more on the creation and implementation of innovations than on the description of a particular packaged innovation or a particular set of innovations that the external change agents want the schools to adopt. Hummell considers such a design to be a transactional model, because the external agents maintain a consultant role for the client teachers in schools; it also may be called an aggregation model, because the school provides a cadre of internal change agents who work with both the external agents and the school staff generally to effect change.

The lack of a widely held working theory of diffusion, noted earlier, has been an important factor in the dispersal of research energy over a wide array of topics. In addition, most diffusion models seem to be either mere descriptions of experiments in diffusion or minimal attempts to generalize from a limited number of cases. The main body of literature pertaining to diffusion focuses on variables and their relationships, and a large proportion of the work done in this area is confined to data correlation with all its characteristic limitations. It is on this somewhat unpromising foundation that current diffusion studies rest.

DIFFUSION RESEARCH VARIABLES AND HYPOTHESES

Most diffusion studies deal with hypotheses that are of the form X varies directly as Y, or X varies inversely as Y. In the majority of cases, the dependent variable Y represents rate of adoption, or some analogous or closely related concept. It is theoretically possible for an innovation to be quickly adopted but slowly diffused (that is, the period from awareness to adoption may be short in some schools, but in the communication across schools, it may be particularly slow), so that it is essential to specify clearly the nature of the dependent variable and the exact means of data collection. The independent variable X ranges from cost or cost-benefit through compatibility, complexity, and other characteristics of the innovations, to innovativeness, openness, and the characteristics of the adopter. The most prominent independent variable in diffusion literature generally is some form of cost. It may be dollar cost or manpower cost; but whatever the case, it reduces to a specific quantity of a factor closely related to dollars.

In his early studies on educational innovation, Mort identifies cost-per-pupil as a critical variable (Carlson, 1965, p. 61). The rationale here is that school systems with a higher cost-per-pupil are more innovative; they not only introduce more innovations, but also adopt on a faster schedule. Mort's assumptions are disputed by Carlson (1965, p. 62), who provides data indicating the lack of relationship between cost-per-pupil and rate of innovation.

The cost-per-pupil variable must be distinguished from the concept of profitability or cost-benefit. Cost-per-pupil is a measure of the affluence of the community combined with its willingness to pay for education. The concept of profitability or cost-benefit concerns a specific innovation and its economic advantage to the user as related to its cost to the user. In the case of agricultural innovation, the user and decision maker is the farmer. In the case of educational innovation, it is not clear who is the user, nor is it clear who is the decision maker. Early educational studies were based on the assumption that the school superintendent was the decision maker, and the benefits and costs were related to him. More recently, it has become necessary to regard adoption decisions as being dispersed to school and classroom units, and the student is now recognized, in a real sense, as the ultimate user and beneficiary.

Miles (1964, ch. 25) has indicated that diffusion rates in educational systems may be slower than those found in industrial, agricultural, or medical systems because of the absence of valid scientific research findings and the lack of an economic incentive to adopt the innovations. He identifies cost as the factor most likely to affect the adoption and continued use of innovations. He also suggests that it must be possible for the school community to purchase or pay for the innovation; and at the same time, it must be possible for someone to make a profit on the manufacture and distribution of it. There must be an economic advantage for some individual or group; and not only must the economic advantage be well specified, but it must also be clear to whom the advantage accrues.

The cost issue is considered by Rogers (1962, p. 124) and other rural sociologists under the term *relative advantage*. Rogers identifies it as the primary characteristic of an innovation, and he relates it to economic profitability. He also sees a significant relationship between economic and social crises and innovation adoption rates. For example, there is a noticeable reduction in adoption rate during an economic depression and an increase in rate following it. Educational writers have observed the role of crisis in the sputnik event. In this case, there was an unusually active period of innovation immediately following the satellite launching; and the rate of introduction of innovations more than doubled within fifteen months during the crisis period (Brickell, 1961, p. 18).

The compatibility variable is identified as the second most prominent characteristic of an innovation. In this case, Rogers (1962, p. 126) states that an idea that is not compatible with the cultural norms of a social system will not be adopted as rapidly as an idea that is compatible. For example, beef production cannot be adopted as an agricultural innovation in India because it is not compatible with the country's cultural values. Similarly, in many primitive societies, there are taboos that prevent the introduction of such beneficial innovations as boiled water, the wheel, and fluoridation.

The effect of taboos, behavioral norms, and general expectations is similar in education. The teaching of evolution was not well received in the Bible Belt of the United States, and it is unlikely that a twelve-month school will be viewed favorably as an innovative idea in typical schools in Canada. Gottlieb and Brookover (1966) have suggested that there must be a generalized climate of acceptance of change or a commitment to norms generally favorable to the acceptance of change. It is reasonable to suggest, then, that conformity or compatibility can be manipulated through the planned evolution of a generalized climate for change. Of course, such a climate does not eliminate variations in compatibility or conformity among innovations; indeed, these variations can be expected to affect the adoption. But the general climate may be a superordinate factor intervening generally on the issue of compatibility. This hypothesis and others similar to it have led to the development of a number of climate-measurement scales, such as Benvenuti's scale, Lerner's modernism scale, Copp's index, and Hobb's scale (Rogers, 1962, p. 63).

Compatibility is related also to relative advantage or cost. Dollars, or dollar costs, identify a dimension that is clearly defined and highly valued by most people. In one sense, the inability or unwillingness of a potential adopter to pay the cost of an innovation may be considered a lack of compatibility. The dollar dimension is just one of many dimensions in the value system possessed by an adopter. Another dimension or cluster of dimensions is religion. An adopter's religion can make one innovation desirable and another unacceptable. There are many dimensions to the adopter's value system, and compatibility must be recognized as a relevant factor for each one. It is also necessary to know how the dollar dimension relates to the other dimensions if the relationship between cost and compatibility is to be explained in a meaningful way.

Complexity is the third of the independent variables ranked by Rogers. Kivlin (1960) and others have documented a negative relationship between complexity and rate of adoption. In its most general sense, complexity is related to the first two variables. The more complex ideas are, the more difficult they are to learn and thus the more costly in terms of time and effort expended. Some ideas that are complex, however, may appeal to some innovators because high complexity may be compatible with the individual's taste. In such cases, compatibility is confounded with complexity.

Two other variables that Rogers associates with innovations and their rate of adoption are divisibility and communicability. In the case of divisibility, it is useful to apply an innovation on a small scale before a large-scale commitment is made. At first, only a proportion of the total innovation or a certain number of units may be introduced, or the number of classes or communities trying it out may be limited. In either case, divisibility will result in a dollar saving. Communicability refers to the relative ease with which the innovative idea can be communicated to potential adopters. The easier it is to communicate, the more rapid will be its adoption, given a positive relationship with the variables of complexity, compatibility, and cost.

The next array of variables concerns the innovator, the innovative unit, and the innovative system as opposed to the innovation itself. The primary characteristic has been considered already in the discussion of compatibility: a generalized compatibility or climate for change or a state of innovativeness tends to characterize potential adopters who in fact adopt or adopt early.

Adopters or potential adopters can be classified according to the amount of the generalized innovativeness that they possess. Rogers uses the word *innovators*, Cocking uses *lighthouses*, and Mort uses *pioneers* to describe the most innovative group; the second group are called early adopters, spark plugs, and leaders by Coleman, Ross, and Mort respectively; early majority, late majority, and laggards describe the remaining categories (Rogers, 1962, p. 150).

The concept of openness seems to be related to generalized innovativeness. It intimately concerns the characteristics of people and their mechanisms for communication. Such terms as *cosmopoliteness* and *localiteness* of the opinion leaders are related to openness in the sense that the gatekeepers or opinion leaders must be open to ideas from the outside world as well as to new ideas from within the local community. If a full variety of possible innovations is to be considered and if the innovations considered are to have the kind of thorough documentation that enhances their potential for success, then a high degree of openness is essential. Fullan and

Eastabrook (1970, p. 10) have hypothesized that the greater the exchange between the school and its various constituencies regarding formulation of goals, the greater is the school's innovativeness. In the Fullan–Eastabrook hypothesis, the emphasis is not only on openness, but on goal orientation as well.

An issue related to openness is the pattern of communication. It seems that there are specific characteristics of this pattern that can facilitate or impede diffusion. Lippitt (1967, p. 311) identifies communication from teachers to principal as critical and yet often lacking in real situations. He also suggests that horizontal communication across teachers is critical, and he points to norms of privatism as a serious hindrance to innovation and diffusion. Inward communication from the producers of innovations to the adoption system is obviously vital to diffusion; but in most school systems, the mechanism for such inward communication is lacking or at best faulty. In the early educational studies documented by Mort, the focus of attention was on the superintendent (director of education in Ontario); later studies by Carlson (1965) focused on his communications within the group of superintendents. Through the use of sociometric plotting of superintendents' relationships within their peer groups, Carlson (1965, pp. 17–21) found that the more popular superintendents tended to adopt faster, thus supporting communication as a facilitator to adoption. In the context of decision making in the 1970s, communication patterns among decision makers should be plotted at the lower echelons.

Fullan and Eastabrook (1970, p. 17) have hypothesized that the greater the shared influence in decision making, the greater is the school's innovativeness. They point to studies by Bell (1967), Abbott (1965), and Miles (1965), indicating that a formal bureaucracy with its hierarchy of decision making, formalized rules, downward procedural specification, and impersonality are dysfunctional for the purpose of accomplishing tasks that require high discretion. Since many educational decisions fit in the high-discretion category, the Fullan–Eastabrook proposition is of some significance.

SOME BASIC PROBLEMS

Perhaps the most basic of all problems relating to diffusion of educational innovations is the acute lag between development and adoption. Rogers (1962) attributes some of the lag in education, and perhaps in other fields as well, to the lack of integration of research information on the process of diffusion. Not until the 1960s was there any serious attempt to bring together diffusion research information from anthropology, rural sociology, medical sociology, industrial sociology, educational sociology, and communications. By 1967, there had been considerable cross-fertilization among these disciplines, and Miles specified the following list (Watson, 1967, p. 26) of needed social inventions that he thought would serve to reduce the lag:

1. Methods for goal clarification. There is a need for precision and beyond that a kind of consensus, so that incompatibilities are identified and resolved.

2. Goal-movement assessment tools. These apply to day-to-day short-run consequences.

3. Improved mechanisms for feedback from children. Both direct and indirect communication from children to adults are to be tapped.

4. Easy-to-use adult behavioral measures (such as a Likert scale).

5. Free space for personnel and organizational development. This refers to released time, sabbaticals, and the facility to use free time.

6. Change managing units. This is a person or personnel group who performs a similar function to that of the county agent in agriculture.

7. Interagency linking mechanisms.

8. Personnel development units in programs.

9. Role supports for the superintendent.

10. Conflict management education.

11. Interrole and intergroup confrontation mechanisms.

12. Environmental scanning roles.

13. Board development mechanisms.

Since 1970, some of these needed social inventions have existed in a more or less usable form. How these are available for use in the Peterborough Project and how the other diffusion literature applies to the diffusion model will be seen from our description of the activities of the Trent Valley Centre and the Project in the next chapter.

CHAPTER 3
Application of diffusion literature

The concept of diffusion is central to the Peterborough Project, for diffusion is the target of its major objectives. It is appropriate, then, to examine the Project in the light of the diffusion literature reviewed in the previous chapter.

Innovations introduced by the Project may be processes, material products, or both; hence, the development of innovations may involve the modification of the behavior of people (mostly teachers), the selective adaptation of materials (such as books, notes, and films), or both. In all instances, the proposed innovation is modified through various stages to a user-readiness stage. Modifications that take place in the last stages of field testing are classified as field development. At this point, students who are presumably typical are taught in "typical" classrooms by "typical" teachers in "typical" communities. The teacher-training activities that must accompany the installation of innovations are not considered to be part of this field development stage.

THE ADOPTION PROCESS The five stages in the adoption process identified by Rogers (1962) and the ten identified by Watson (1967) can be quickly recognized for all innovations introduced under the Project. Watson's list is perhaps the more sensitive of the two, in this context, since it was developed specifically with a focus on education.

The awareness or sensing stage is, of course, critical to the initiation of any innovation, but it is a delicate phase to plan and carry out. In education, a large quantity of specialized manpower apparently is needed to bring teachers and school officials to a point of receptivity to information about innovations. The strategy employed within the Project involves the allocation of a substantial amount of specialized manpower – OISE staff, principals, and specially trained teachers.

Whether or not this manpower allocation is adequate and whether or not its deployment is efficient are questions that remain to be answered.

At the interest stage – comprised of screening, diagnosing, and inventing – the aware individual reacts to the innovative idea and is led to find out more about it. Screening is particularly important in the educational context. The teacher or principal receives many communications concerning innovations, and it is necessary for him to select among them to determine which merit further attention. In the Project schools, some assistance in the screening process is provided by the OISE personnel. The subsequent stage of diagnosing involves the careful study by the teacher of a potentially useful innovation; he matches it to his goals and assesses the suitability of the innovation in its present form. In the inventing stage, he creates adaptations that will be required before the innovation can be considered for use in the setting intended.

Evaluation involves two processes: weighing and decision. Some evaluation occurs during screening and diagnosing, but the main evaluation stage that leads directly to a decision involves a study of evaluative data and careful consideration of all relevant issues. In the Project, data pertaining to programs under consideration are available to the schools that are contemplating their adoption. Some data originate in pilot trials and some come from the five Core Group schools. As later Study Groups are formed and later innovation decisions are made for these schools, evaluation data will be available that pertain directly to schools in the same school district.

In educational innovation, a number of trials or pretests are necessary prior to adoption of a new program or tool. It is common for the first preliminary trial to contain faults or cause problems that may not recur in later operating stages. The reason for this is the factor of teacher performance; in nearly all cases, the pilot trial performance of the teacher is different from the second and virtually all subsequent performances.

The evaluation of educational innovations is not a simple matter. There are many factors to be considered, and often these are difficult to quantify. Pilot or preliminary trials are therefore intended, not to achieve a summative evaluation of a finished product, but to provide a formative evaluation leading to further trials that incorporate revisions based on these early data. The Project's commitment to evaluation is weighted heavily in favor of formative as opposed to summative evaluation.

There is little in the literature on educational innovation that describes or classifies the role of agents of change. The Boston Strategy, as we have seen, discusses change agents under two categories: internal agents and external agents. In the Philadelphia Plan, the change agents are called intermediaries, and they are drawn from leadership positions within the target community – that is, the emphasis is on internal agents. The Peterborough Project depends equally upon internal and external change agents, and its overall strategy is focused on extending the number of the former. For example, the Trent Valley Centre, as an external agent, worked extensively with the staff of two schools to develop criterion-referenced evaluation instruments for two programs. This work involved substantial amounts of teacher training that now allows those teachers to carry on independently with other programs in the original schools and in other schools where they are teaching.

DIFFUSION VARIABLES The dependent variable in diffusion studies generally pertains to rate of adoption; the independent variable presumably is a manipulable, or at least measurable and predictable, factor.

In considering the dependent variable, it is necessary to distinguish between the adoption period for a single adopting unit and an area's rate of adoption from the time of the first adoption to the time of the last within a population of potential adopters. The period of adoption for the Project is estimated in months, and the estimate is used to determine the appropriate time of sensitization or goal orientation that will yield a decision by February or March in any given year.[1]

COST VARIABLES In education studies, it is very difficult to estimate the costs of innovations, and it is therefore difficult to define the precise relationship that exists between costs and rates of adoption. In the experience of the Peterborough Project, the two have been found to be highly interdependent. On the one hand, the cost of an innovation may significantly affect its rate of adoption; for example, an excessively expensive innovation may tend to experience a modest adoption rate. On the other hand, the rate of adoption may influence the actual operating cost of an innovation as opposed to its estimated pre-adoption cost; for example, widespread adoption may greatly reduce the material investment in a new program by effecting substantial economies of scale. Similarly, the cost of creating a climate for change cannot be accurately estimated for large-scale diffusion, because the present supply of free or voluntary manpower may be exhausted and it may be necessary to release large numbers of teachers from their normal teaching duties. It is clear, then, that under present circumstances, the cost of educational innovations within the Project cannot be estimated with any degree of precision.

It is even more difficult to assess the benefits of educational innovations. Few, if any, standardized tests correspond directly to the goals of existing programs; hence,

[1]This particular period has been selected for reasons of convenience: it is the time when educational budgets are decided for the following school year.

they are likely to be of limited use in assessing program benefits. The more recent criterion-referenced or domain-referenced tests will overcome this problem, but they can deal only with criteria that are clearly specified and observable. At present, all that can be clearly described and observed is cognitive achievement performance. It remains for future educational technicians to introduce the measurement devices that will describe precisely the many other results, positive or negative, associated with specific innovations.

Even if the precise costs and benefits of innovations could be accurately specified, there would remain the very serious problem of incentive or relative advantage. In education, there are no easy answers to the crucial questions of who saves money and who benefits. It appears that in the case of some responsibly devised innovations, society in general stands to benefit as a result of long-range benefits to the student. In such a case, however, there is no compelling incentive on the part of the teacher, the principal, the superintendent, or the student to accept the innovation if it happens to be contrary to his tastes. There is a trend presently under way in the Project to introduce financial decision-making responsibility at the level of the local school in a much broader sense than ever before. One of the problems in the past has been that the school has maintained a child–parent relationship with the central administration with regard to finances. This general practice in education seems to have led to a situation where the schools plead with the central administration for whatever they require. If more responsibility is placed with the users of the innovation, more effective and relevant decision making should result.

An incentive device that has emerged recently in the United States is performance contracting, whereby a contractor is paid for getting a teaching job done. The misuses of performance contracting have been documented elsewhere (see Estes, 1971). They are no surprise to Ontario educators because of Ontario's unique educational experiences in the period of the 1880s. At that time, "payment by results" was practiced in Ontario (and nowhere else apparently) and the effects were disastrous by the time the practice was discarded. In the Ontario case, the payment was to the school or to the teacher. In order to avoid such misuses, an incentive scheme for teachers should be created that has a different basis of operation. At present, there is no rationale available in the Project situation to overcome these problems.

COMPATIBILITY Compatibility is the next most important factor in adoption decisions. An innovation that is not compatible with the cultural norms of the social system either will not be adopted at all, or will be adopted very slowly and by a small minority of potential adopters. The issue of compatibility arises in various subtle ways in the Project, and there is an equally subtle resolution of such issues. There has been no careful documentation to date of sociological characteristics of relevant county schools in connection with the Project or the Trent Valley Centre; those estimates that have been suggested, however, indicate that there are no atypical characteristics in either the positive or the negative direction on any of the major variables in the socio-economic domain. (See, for example, the SES data reported in chapter 7.)

One of the basic policies of the Project program is that classroom teachers should share in decision-making responsibility pertaining to curriculum and instruction. This policy, which originated in the Hall–Dennis Report (*Living and learning*, 1968), has been faithfully implemented in all schools in the Core Group, and it seems that it will be implemented in decisions affecting the Study Group as well. Of course, some principals, superintendents, and directors of education do not wish to delegate responsibility for such critical decisions. Nevertheless, the administration has accepted the policy insofar as it applies to schools in the Core Group and the Study Group, and Core Group principals also have delegated responsibility to classroom teachers. A problem of compatibility may arise at some point in the future, when unsympathetic principals are encouraged to participate in later Study Group activities; they may find it difficult to share their responsibilities with teachers, and resist doing so. By the time such individuals find their way into Study Groups, however, changing norms in the community may facilitate a change of attitude on their part.

One clear advantage of the Project's policy of delegated responsibility is that the classroom teacher is as well informed as any individual or group in ensuring that innovations selected for his school are compatible with the values of the school community. The degree to which a teacher is influenced by the judgment of students and parents in forming his impressions of the value system of the school varies from individual to individual; but in all cases, there is a mechanism for the participation of parents in the establishment of school goals, and presumably this mechanism has a positive effect on the teacher's perception of what needs to be done.

Through the study of reports such as *Living and learning* (1968) and through planning sessions that deal with school goals, the teachers in the Core schools have been stimulated or sensitized to the point where a positive climate for change is in evidence. In some schools, the staff have selected changes that depend heavily on staff production of new instructional material and new topic sequences. Other schools have pursued a course that seems almost diametrically opposite, choosing to solve their priority problems through the use of highly structured materials, such as Individually Prescribed Instruction and the Conceptual Skills Program. While neither of these packaged programs is wholly compatible with the spirit of parts of the

Hall–Dennis Report, the use of them is consistent with the document's main recommendation, namely, that teachers should be involved in curriculum and instruction decisions and that in making such decisions they should be responsive to both students and parents. This compatibility with the Hall–Dennis Report on the issue of teacher decision making is most important to the present discussion, because it is this feature that ensures or tends to ensure the compatibility of the selected innovations within the school setting.

The use of volunteer assistance in the ongoing activities of the Project schools raises another set of compatibility issues. Where parents have replaced teachers, there is considerable reluctance on the part of a few principals and a number of teachers to lend support (Hedges, 1972). The degree to which local norms will change may depend to some extent on the success of a particular doctoral study that is designed to identify the priority issues in connection with parental involvement and to design a program to optimize the benefits to parents, teachers, and students through the volunteer activities of parents. Preliminary indications are that the reluctance of principals and teachers to utilize volunteer parents is without rational foundation, as is the reluctance of some teachers to introduce highly structured programs.

COMPLEXITY It is clear that for Project innovations, the complexity variable is closely related to cost and compatibility. The creation of a climate for change is a highly complex and costly task, requiring a considerable amount of time for thought and communication on the part of a number of teachers, principals, and external specialists. Highly complex innovations, such as IPI, require considerable training time, for the school principal must take two weeks of his vacation time or two weeks away from his school to participate in the basic training workshop. Whether or not complexity can be considered independently of cost and compatibility is not of major concern in the Project. What is important is that virtually all of the innovations contemplated within the Project must be considered complex and hence difficult to adopt.

OTHER VARIABLES A considerable amount of study has been devoted to the problem of communication within and across systems, and the relationship of communication to the dependent variable. When complex tasks are involved, horizontal communication is superior to hierarchical or bureaucratic communication. This is an important point in the planned relationship between Core Group schools and Study Group schools. One might infer that communication would automatically originate with the Core schools and would be passed on to the Study schools; thus, the relationship between the two groups would be hierarchical. This pattern was anticipated early in 1970/71, and steps were taken to ensure that horizontal rather than vertical communication was established. In particular, some Study schools were encouraged to pursue promising innovations that they had identified on their own and with the Trent Valley Centre's help, but that were not in the roster of components of the existing program. Also, the initiative for communication between Study schools and Core schools was consciously left to the Study schools. In spite of these changes, there is some residual negative feeling, and in part this may be a valid reflection of the fact that the Core school principals and their staff are in possession of many ideas, processes, materials, and feelings that merit consideration by the Study schools. It is to be hoped that the essential vitality of self-renewal that characterizes the Core schools will be generated by the Study schools and perceived by them, and rightly so, as their own. Nevertheless, a change from the Study Group–Core Group type of structure has been effected. This process is described in chapter 4.

A further listing of independent variables related to rate of adoption will be left to a later report on the Project. One other feature of the literature that warrants attention at this point is Miles's list of needed social inventions (Watson, 1967, p. 26). The first need is for methods of goal clarification. Although goal identification in the school system and goal clarification within the Project schools can be commended as being more advanced than those in most schools and school systems, a considerable amount of work remains to be done, both at the theoretical level and at the practical level of the schools in the community. The second priority need is for goal-movement assessment tools. Within the Project, almost the full time of the Development Officer is devoted to activities that come under this heading. Criterion-referenced test items, criterion-referenced social behavior, and attitude measures have been generated to assess the short-run consequences of various treatments.

Improved mechanisms for feedback from children represent a long-standing need that is not likely to be adequately met in the foreseeable future. In this program, one principal has devoted fifty to seventy days of effort to the construction, application, and analysis of data that deal with communication from children to adults (Montgomery, 1970). The fourth priority need is for easy-to-use adult behavioral measures, and the fifth for free space for personnel and organizational development. The project depends on released time for teachers and space for them to work from the beginning of the program, and this is still a high priority need.

A change agent or change managing units constitute the sixth listed priority need. The Trent Valley Centre has been perceived as an answer or the answer to this need during the first years of its operation. The seventh need is for interagency linking mechanisms, and again it is related to the role of the Trent Valley Centre. It should not be assumed, however, that no other interagency linking mechanisms are required, since resources of the Trent Valley Centre are extremely limited in relation to the magnitude of its task in Region 9.

Personnel development units in programs are another concern of the Trent Valley Centre. Some of the activities directed to this need are teacher training for Conceptual Skills, Individually Prescribed Instruction, the Ontario Teachers' Federation Science Program, and planning sessions for principals leading to an understanding of the climate for change.

The ninth, tenth, eleventh, and thirteenth priority needs are for role supports for the superintendent, conflict management education, interrole and intergroup confrontation mechanisms, and board development mechanisms. The Trent Valley Centre recognizes these needs and would support attempts to satisfy them on the part of groups internal or external to the school system, except that present manpower limitations require only passing acknowledgment of the problems. The twelfth priority need is for environmental scanning roles; in this area, the Trent Valley Centre provides a number of services to the schools that involve it in the scanning of potentially useful components for the various school programs.

One further social invention that can be proposed by the Trent Valley Centre as a priority need is a mechanism to inform parents, teachers, principals, administrators, scholars, and research and development officials of the general range of manpower and dollar costs that are required to be extended over time in order to achieve widespread adoption of demonstrably beneficial school innovations. The program plans outlined above and scheduled in subsequent chapters will cost much more in terms of manpower and their related dollars than the current budget figures reflect. The high costs result from organizational and social inertia, which may be a service to society when it protects against unwarranted changes in direction or velocity, but which must be overcome when valid and highly desirable alternative directions for education need to be taken.

CHAPTER 4

The diffusion process

Although the installation of a climate for change in schools is central to the Project, neither the method of installation nor the climate itself is a feature that is easily described. Nevertheless, it is essential that these terms be clarified. Perhaps this is best done by example. First, we will briefly discuss commonly used methods that are intended to create a climate for change, but fail to do so; then we will identify some of the indicators of such a climate.

    It is a common practice of some academics to spend a portion of their time giving talks to groups of educators about current problems and their solution. The intended purpose of such lectures undoubtedly is to instill in the audience a feeling of dissatisfaction with the present state of affairs and to point them in the "right" direction. Presumably, this brief exposure provides the impetus that enables the practitioner to overcome "minor" operational problems and bring about change. If such a strategy were effective, virtually all schools by now would be beehives of innovative activity, since most staff have heard inspirational speeches on many occasions. The fact remains, however, that substantially fewer than all schools are involved in meaningful innovation. This suggests that a disproportionate amount of time has been spent on generating answers to problems, as opposed to finding ways of implementing the answers, and it also suggests a failure to recognize the magnitude and complexity of the task of implementing change in schools.

    It is often implied that there is a very large group of educational practitioners with problems and a very small, exclusive group of educational researchers who have the answers. Nothing could be further from the truth. The answers generated by educational researchers to problems in the world of the practicing teacher and administrator are few. While the special knowledge and scientific tools of the educational researcher make him *potentially* valuable to the practitioner, realization of this potential will not occur through isolated, infrequent, and one-way communication channels.

Other common methods used for introducing change fail to recognize the total school as the critical educational unit in any decision resulting in effective change. Take, for example, the efforts made in some parts of the United States to have schools accept and make use of one highly developed computer-assisted instruction package. It was introduced to some teachers in the schools through extensive workshops designed to enable them to implement the program in their classes. The teachers, however, were directly responsible to the principal, who often did not understand what was being done and as a result failed to provide the type of support required. This situation differs only in some details from the common practice of imposing innovation from higher-level administrative authority without full involvement in the decision by the teachers and principals who must implement the innovation. It is a basic premise of the Peterborough Project that a change must be felt by or created in those who have the task of implementing the change if the problems of implementation are to be understood in a manner conducive to solution, and if the change agents are to be sufficiently committed to endure the extra burden of implementation.

The existence of a climate for change in a school is evident in the actions of the teachers, the principal, and quite often, although less noticeably, the students. A climate for change exists where teachers are prepared to rearrange their classroom schedules in order to meet regularly to discuss a common problem. Such meetings are typically characterized by an open admission of evident weaknesses in the existing program. The ability of teachers to do this is based on both the security and the feeling of responsibility that is attached to the role of a prime change agent. There is also a commitment to action as well as discussion of these problems. A climate for change also often exists in schools where the principal gives the teachers' planning group complete control over their own budget, where he may occasionally be outvoted on important program matters, and where he is guided by the decision of the majority, or where a teacher can refuse, on rational grounds, to implement an innovation strongly favored by the principal without fear or certain knowledge of reprisals. A climate for change probably exists as well where a principal elicits the consent of the administration, parents, and the public transport system for a timetable change that will give teachers the opportunity to meet for cooperative planning.

Each of these circumstances can be found in the schools of the Peterborough Project, and many more emerge as the staff, and sometimes the parents, talk to visitors to the Project and try to explain what it is about. It is important to realize that these examples are not magic solutions that, imposed on a school, will by themselves produce a climate for change. Rather, they are symptoms or manifestations of a dynamic process that underlies the operation of the entire innovational program.

The generation of a climate for change and the implementation of change in the Core schools of the Project have been designated as Phase 1 of an ongoing diffusion activity. The replication of this program throughout all the elementary schools of the province represents an enormous, costly, and time-consuming task. For example, it would require all the manpower of the Trent Valley Centre and an equal amount of assistance from the central office of OISE for a period of ten years to cover the elementary schools in one county alone. Consequently, Phase 2 has emerged as a totally different array of activities from Phase 1 with regard to personnel involvement. The ultimate purpose of the program, however, in terms of its impact on students, is the same as it is in Phase 1. Again, the objective is to instill a climate for change within the schools and subsequently to introduce innovations for trial, assessment, and adoption or rejection. The essential strategy proposed for Phase 2 that distinguishes it from a replication of Phase 1 is its use of county personnel from the Core schools and the administrative staff in a communication network extending into the radial schools. It is the communication network that in time expedites the diffusion of the climate for change, as well as the more robust components of innovative programs, beyond the Core schools to the various other schools of the county.

The 1970/71 school year gave rise to progress in the establishment of a communication network in two distinct but interdependent ways. A group of radial schools, known as the Study Group, was envisioned as the first of a series of concentric rings of innovating schools surrounding the Core Group. On the basis of the experience of the Study Group schools after working together for one year, a modified plan for diffusion in 1971/72 was created that was designed to achieve the major purposes of the concentric ring model, and at the same time to overcome the problems encountered and foreseen by the Core and Study groups in implementing such a plan. The following discussion concerns, first, the establishment of the Study Group and the conceptual framework within which it functions; and second, the modified plan for 1971/72 diffusion activities.

ESTABLISHING THE STUDY GROUP   The original six (Core) schools in the program were primarily self-selecting, and they would be considered innovators according to Rogers's (1962) categorization. Some of the principals in these schools, however, were selected by central board administrative decision as opposed to self-selection. There is no written account of administrative purpose in making these decisions. For the twelve Study Group schools, the selection was again a combination of self-selection and administrative preference. These schools may be considered early adopters according to Rogers's classification.

The Core schools consist of one separate school and five public elementary city schools. The Study Group comprises two separate schools (one city and one rural) and ten public elementary schools (eight in or near Peterborough and two thirty miles from Peterborough). It is important to note that one of these Study Group schools was originally in the self-selecting group of Core schools, but in the first two-month period the staff decided to drop out, thus relieving themselves of what they considered to be the burden of innovation that they felt was a commitment of their involvement in the Project. Their rejoining the Project later as members of the Study Group was a result of an improved climate for change brought about by unspecified factors.

The Study Group was formed for the purpose of testing the feasibility of replicating the Core Group study activities on a larger scale. The meetings of the Study Group principals began in 1970, and they were held weekly or biweekly at the TVC office. After the group had met several times, and had wrestled with the problem of their own purposes as a group and the general purposes of education in their schools, they asked the TVC staff how they could organize to capitalize on the Centre's manpower to the optimum degree. It was proposed that a strategy be adopted in which the twelve schools would be the first diffusion link and a later array of schools would become the secondary target population, linking back to the first Study Group schools.

Subsequent to the decision to approve in principle the idea of diffusion, the first stage in the Study Group meetings was to search for problems, and this led back to specification of the goals for each individual school. The study of goals in turn led to a serious discussion of who should establish the goals and through what mechanism. It was a key project component that the major curriculum decisions should be made by the teachers in the light of their sensitivity to the needs of students within the environment of the school.

Goal Identification

Each of the Study Group schools and in fact all the schools in the county have embarked on a broad study of school goals. While this process is under way among teachers and principals in the school units, some of the Study Group have focused on a detailed specification of goals. This is intended to lead to a further study of various devices designed to measure the attainment of goals by students in schools. To date, as a direct result of this study, two county-wide conferences have been held on evaluation for principals. The conferences have prompted the initiation of a five-day summer workshop on evaluation that is attended by principals, vice-principals, and some high-school department heads.

The search for problems to be solved is partly rational and partly accidental. Although organized to the extent already described, it is somewhat accidental in that the wide variety of pressures felt by teachers and principals in the Study schools cannot be cataloged and measured in any precise way. It is clear that the authority to identify problems has been given over to the schools by the administrators of the county system, and also that the principals have agreed to a commitment to pass on the decision-making authority to their staff. The extent to which this latter commitment will be fulfilled probably varies from school to school, but the fact that teachers feel that they possess authority and are expected to respond to it has been well documented (McGill & Skinner, 1970). It is true also that in some schools, the priority listing of problems has been organized and a systematic scheme for attacking the problems adopted. In all instances, the relationship between the problems identified and the goals of the school has been clearly stated.

Schools, Problems, and Solutions
Once a problem area has been firmly established as worthy of attention and of the highest priority, the search for solutions formally begins. There are, of course, informal searches for solutions while the various problems are being identified by staff and principals, and sometimes solutions are found before the problems are clearly specified. The phase that of necessity precedes problem identification or formulation of a solution is the general awareness that problems may exist. In the Study Group, the awareness has been brought on by the regular meetings of the Study Group and by the meetings that Study Group principals hold with their staff. For some staff, awareness has come quickly, if it was not there beforehand. For others, it is still emerging after a year of work. In the latter case, the next step in creating awareness has been to encourage the principal and various members of his staff to visit Core schools or other schools where they may see operating solutions to existing problems and talk to trusted colleagues about the whole rationale for change.

In some schools, the decision to search for a solution is a group decision involving the entire staff; in other schools, it is an individual decision; but in most cases, it is a subgroup of the entire staff that pursues the solution. Early decisions to search for solutions in the Core schools have been based on such considerations as low school scores on the standard test administered across the county (Canadian Test of Basic Skills). In the case of some of the Study Group schools, these same standardized test scores have prompted a number of preliminary investigations. In other instances, the principal and staff have become aware of needed changes through informal liaison with the principal or staff of Core schools, or through participation in graduate studies programs at OISE and at the University of Ottawa. Also, some of the sales representatives from educational manufacturing concerns have stimulated thought on the part of teachers and principals that has led them to a careful study of various packaged solutions to problems.

Where interpretation of standardized test scores has been used as a basis for identifying priority problems, the TVC staff have been involved in clarifying interpretations of score data. One positive result of the meetings concerning the use of standardized test data has been the general swing on the part of principals and teachers toward acceptance of domain-referenced or criterion-referenced tests as an essential tool in evaluation of both curriculum change and student progress. The limitations of standardized tests are well known from the theoretical point of view, and they have been recognized increasingly by Project staff.

Study Group Innovations
One school has undertaken a search for a solution to its priority problem of science; this involves careful study, through the offices of the TVC, of many available science programs. Many procedural solutions, such as those affecting released time for teachers, have been described at Study Group meetings and in visits to Core schools. The use of volunteer parents as a component of this particular array of solutions has been an area of special study within the TVC and the Niagara Centre, and the TVC has offered many suggestions concerning the problems identified by the schools. The TVC also encourages the participation of regional departmental consultants. These individuals have contributed many useful suggestions and identified innovative practices that can be incorporated in the change process in the Core and Study Group schools. The innovative science program of the Ontario Teachers' Federation is another example of an outside link monitored by the Trent Valley Centre. While the TVC usually creates these links, it also fosters links that are created in other ways. The Centre allocates considerable time and energy to the maintenance of these links on a priority basis, with the most productive receiving the most attention.

In short, it appears that the TVC provides the main link for Core Group and Study Group schools with channels of information about advanced practices. It should be understood, however, that the TVC not only links the schools with innovators and innovative practices within the OISE staff group, but also provides a resource for information about innovations generated across Canada and the United States, and outside North America as well.

The decision to adopt a given solution to an identified educational problem is made in various ways, depending upon the problem and the school. In the case of process decisions concerning the release of teachers from regular duties, the decision is characteristically made by the school principal. His continued willingness to work with the Study Group implies greater likelihood that a solution will be implemented or adopted in his school. It has been a feature of the operation of both the Core Group and the Study Group schools that a staff has the right to dissociate itself from the program if that is the wish of the individuals concerned. No definition of priorities or other technicalities has been specified, and to date only one Study Group school has opted out.[1]

The decision to try specific innovative curriculum materials is characteristically made by the subgroups of staff who will be involved in the implementation of the solution. In some instances, the decision involves all the teachers and all the grades in a division, as in the case of IPI; in other cases, it may involve two or more teachers working in a single grade or in a single subject over a two- or three-grade continuum. The decision to try the Conceptual Skills Program is essentially a joint decision between the kindergarten teacher and the school principal, with either party having effective veto power (see chapters 5 and 7). One of the most significant discussions at a joint meeting of the Core Group and the Study Group concerned the situation where a principal was enthusiastic about the Conceptual Skills Program and his kindergarten teacher was unenthusiastic and, if left to her own devices, unwilling to try it. The principal wanted to consider ways of transferring the teacher so that a more willing replacement could move in. The consensus among the principals was that this would violate the basic policy decision that classroom teachers should have their full share of responsibility for curriculum decisions.

When a decision is made to try a particular innovative program, the teachers who make the decision have been provided beforehand with an opportunity to see the program in operation and to discuss with teachers using it the problems leading to and resulting from its adoption. Also, the teachers are provided with all the evidence, in favor of or against the program, that the principal and the TVC staff can find. For example, principals and teachers who showed an interest in a film on Individually Prescribed Instruction materials subsequently were engaged in a three-hour session conducted by a highly reputable detractor of the program.

Since the cost and cost-benefit factors are vital to ultimate decisions for adoption, there are cost deliberations at all levels from the director of education through to the classroom teacher. The decision to try a particular innovation is bound to involve cost considerations at the teacher level, because each school is required to handle

---

[1]In this case, the principal was involved with teaching duties for all but two half-days per week, so that time to attend Study Group meetings was rarely available.

some of the dollar burden out of its own book budget. At the administration level, dollar considerations are pursued from the point of view of the economic feasibility of ultimate widespread adoption. Where very expensive innovations are under consideration, the cost factor is particularly important; the program may finally be rejected even though large achievement gains would result from its adoption. When a decision is made to try a particular innovation, it is clear that the teachers, the principal, the Board administrators, and the TVC favor trial adoption. Also, it is clear that the dollar costs are not prohibitive and that they are spread among the decision makers in a manner that encourages responsible decisions at all levels, as opposed to decisions that are made on the basis of felt needs that can be satisfied by dollars spent by someone other than the beneficiary.

Implementation of Innovations
Psychological support for the introduction of innovations is generated basically through the dispersal of the decision-making process. In fact, an overloading of decision making at the teacher level may be evident in some of the components of the Project. With the shared decision-making strategy under way, there is an added psychological support benefit accruing at the teacher level that results from the principal's positive endorsement of the innovation. This little component of support is often lacking in the introduction of innovations when the teacher attends a training program that his principal and other members of his staff may never fully understand. In the Project, the classroom teacher is supported by his colleagues within the school, by his principal, and by the administration. He enjoys an added component of support through his liaison with teachers in other schools pursuing similar problems and through his liaison with the TVC. Such an array of psychological support coupled with the dispersal of decision making seems to ensure a high degree of commitment on the part of teachers.

Each imported innovative program that is introduced in the Project has its own particular training program. In the case of IPI, the principals involved engaged in a two-week training program called Research for Better Schools, provided by the Regional Educational Laboratory in Philadelphia. Upon their return from the training workshop, the principals planned a training program for their own staff and implemented it both prior to and during the first weeks of school. The principal, then, is responsible for pretrial and in-service training in that particular program. In the case of Conceptual Skills, the preliminary training of principals and teachers is conducted simultaneously by a staff representative from OISE; in the later, more detailed stages, teachers only are involved. In-service training is provided as well, again by the OISE staff representative. Other imported innovative programs depend on less formal training of teachers; but in each case, some substantial training effort is mounted, and often the TVC staff, in cooperation with the principal and other OISE staff, plan and implement the training program. During the early stages of the Project diffusion plan, the burden of training costs was borne to a large extent by the TVC, but with the agreement on the part of the Board of Education that later training would be a responsibility of the Board or the school involved.

There are two levels of decision making on the dollar issue: the central administration level and the school level. These two levels share responsibilities concerning the substance of innovations, and the nature of the sharing is significant. At the level of the central administration, there has been and continues to be firm acceptance of the general plan to involve teachers in curriculum content decisions and to employ volunteer assistance to a limited degree to release teachers for the purpose of planning change. The administration has been represented on the Core Committee and is represented in the Study Group by an area superintendent; hence, not only is the central administration well informed about the progress of the Project and its various details, but the principals and staff of the schools are aware at each decision-making stage that they are not violating administration policy and are in fact supported in their efforts to improve the schools through change.

The school board is responsible for managing the preparation of teachers for trial implementation of innovations, and the performance of training activities is contracted to the TVC staff or its designates on an unpaid client–consultant basis. The adequacy of the teacher preparation is ultimately the responsibility of the administration, and the characteristic evaluation is conducted (quite informally in this county) through the use of superintendents in school observation. This responsibility is shared, however, by the school principal, as part of his overall responsibility for the school and its staff, and by the TVC, particularly insofar as quality of training relates to matters of curriculum content, evaluation, or other technical matters of special interest to the Centre.

The evaluation data (discussed in detail in chapter 7) serve many purposes in the diffusion process. In the first place, the teachers are involved in the specification of objectives and approval of test items in a way that enhances their involvement in the innovation and its substance. The resulting data are more easily interpreted by classroom teachers, and subsequent classroom activities can be adapted accordingly. The Study Group school staff and their principals also receive evaluation data and analysis concerning the components of the existing innovative programs within the Core schools, so that the decisions they make pertaining to the trial of innovative components are based on empirical data emanating from the immediate environment. In some instances, an innovative practice may justifiably be adopted for trial without adaptation; but in others, the data may encourage Study Group schools to modify the program.

A comprehensive evaluation report of a summative nature incorporates all the data and all the components. Such a report can be used by the administration and OISE budget decision makers to determine the extent of expenditure that should be allocated to the Project in the future.

At present, the Study Group is the first attempt to diffuse the innovations introduced under the Project in the Core schools. In the plan outlined in January 1970 for the 1970/71 operation, it was indicated that other groups would be organized in subsequent years to continue the diffusion of the innovations throughout the county area, throughout Region 9, and perhaps in other parts of the province as well.

A MODIFIED PLAN FOR DIFFUSION   The Project operated within this framework throughout the 1970/71 school year. But both the school-centered nature and the grass-roots approach of the Project, as well as the comparatively small amount of reliable information on successful educational development, dictate that modification in planning should be expected on a continuing basis. These modifications will occur largely in the general structural components of the Project model rather than in the specific forms of the relationship among the schools, the administration, and the TVC.

Initially, the plan called for the introduction of innovations in the Core schools first and in the various Study Group schools second. Now it is evident that a number of innovations will be introduced in the Study Group schools and diffused among them and perhaps back to the Core schools. The need to permit such a departure from the original plan became evident when one of the Study schools became ready to introduce a program that would be of considerable value to other schools in both the Study and the Core groups. The former vertical communication link between the two groups clearly had to become horizontal, and the hierarchical relationship that had existed to date was replaced by a peer structure. The original plan also called for a clustering of Study Group schools around a Core school; the initiative for organizing such clusters was to come from the TVC under the leadership of the Core school. In fact, in the 1970/71 school year, the initiative for clustering or liaison came naturally from the Study Group schools, with some stimulation from the TVC staff. The resulting association was hoped to represent a peer liaison.

A systematic realignment of Study and Core groups has now been formulated and is in the process of becoming functional. Its purpose is to deal effectively with the above issues and several major problems that plagued Project members throughout 1970/71. Because the Core group is a relatively small, easily identified group and because it has existed since the Project began, it has found itself spending increasing amounts of time on matters relating only indirectly to the Project. Such matters have included formulating policy to regulate the growing influx of visitors to the schools, processing requests for outside studies of the Project, and determining the implications of publicity. While decisions on these issues have often been made unilaterally by the Core Group for the sake of expediency, they do have equal impact on the Study Group. This method of decision making is potentially hazardous to the Project on two counts. On the one hand, it consumes time better spent by Core Group schools on substantive curriculum problems; and on the other, it fails to ensure formally that the majority of the Project constituency is in accord with the decisions made and is involved in making the decisions. This problem, combined with the early assumption that the Core Group should assume a paternalistic responsibility for program development in Study Group schools, persists as a source of annoyance to many Project members. While this situation may not seem very serious, similar situations have served to retard interschool cooperation, and the one here potentially retards diffusion among members within the Project. A hierarchical structure is difficult to avoid, but it cannot be allowed to interfere with the basic operation of the Project.

Figure 1 shows the stages of the diffusion process followed by the Project. Stage 4 represents the realigned structure, where the Core and Study groups have joined to form a total Project constituency that includes all present and future Project members. From this inclusive body, four members are chosen who, with one member of the staff of the TVC, form a Liaison Committee. Their term of office is not less than one year. The total Project constituency (the Joint Group) meets periodically but does most of its work in problem or interest groups. These groups are formed whenever two or more schools identify a common problem of high priority. There may be as many of these groups as there are priority problems, and one school may belong to more than one group. When a viable solution has been found to the problem, the group disbands. Because one of the major problems encountered by Study Group principals has been the creation of a climate for change in their schools, it seems likely that one of the interest groups will focus on this issue. Although as yet undecided, participation in this group may become a prerequisite for acceptance of a new school into the Project. This seems to be one potential method of ensuring that the essential ingredient in the Project – teacher responsibility for planning and implementing change – is passed on to new members. It is erroneous to assume that schools that are involved in curriculum development activity are necessarily involved in process or product diffusion. They may never have grappled with more general issues of change and may never have had the opportunity to acquire the

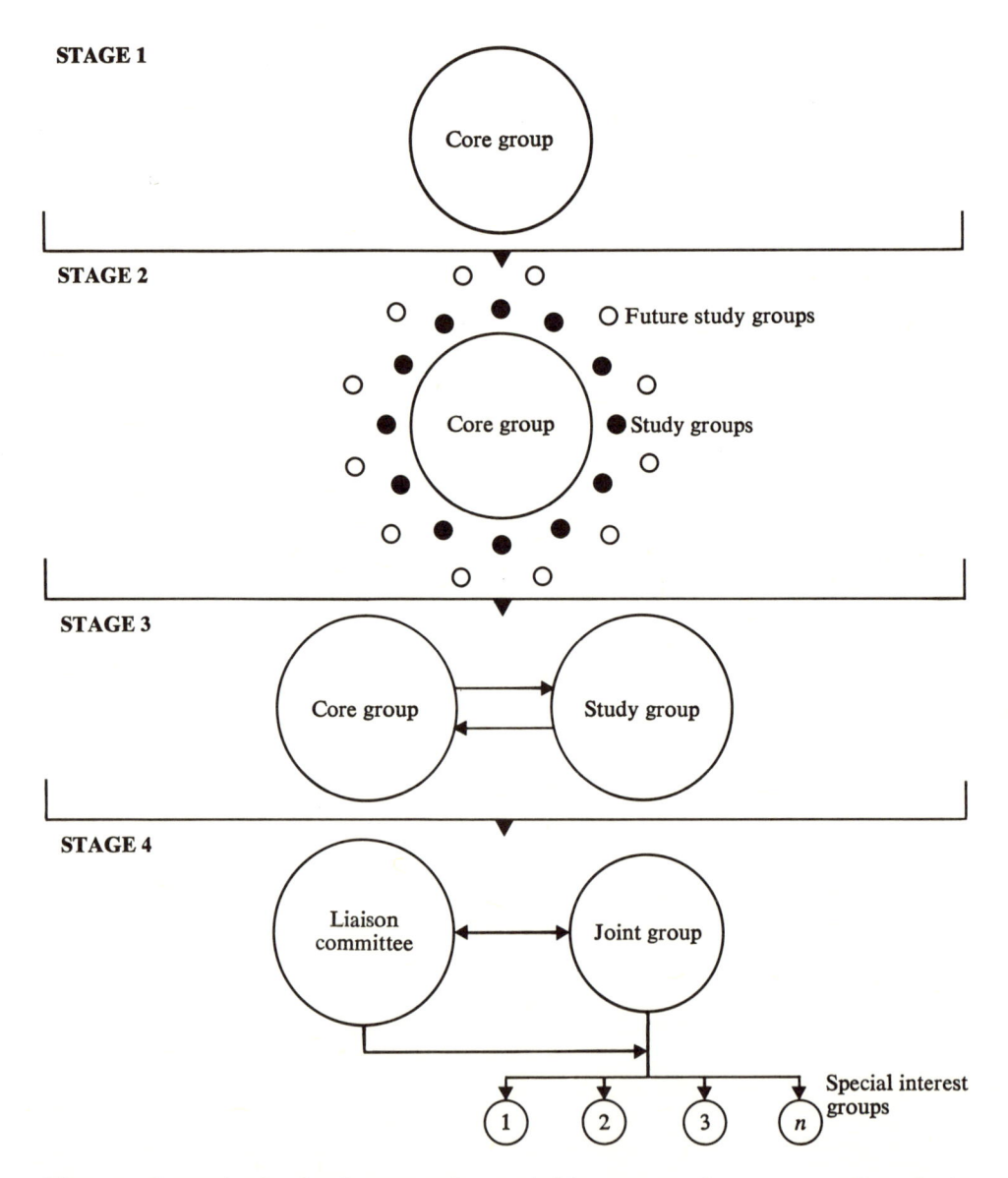

Figure 1. Stages in the development of a workable structure for process and product diffusion among schools in the Project.

skills necessary for curriculum development and implementation.

The general purpose of the Liaison Committee is to facilitate productive group activity. It is not designed to perform executive functions. The specific functions outlined for it at its inception were as follows:

1. To coordinate meetings and exchange of ideas among schools working on similar problems.

2. To coordinate requests for aid (such as materials and personnel) to appropriate sources both inside and outside the Project. A major reason for schools to work in groups when common problems are evident is not only so that they can exchange ideas among themselves, but also so that they form a substantial body for the efficient use of consultative resources. For example, it would be unwise for OISE in general and TVC in particular to respond to *individual* school requests for assistance. Such a response, however, makes a great deal of sense when most of the schools in a county with the same problem make a joint request for assistance. It then becomes economically feasible for a consultative agency to make a contribution with a high probability of positive results.

3. To review requests and administrative problems directed to the Project by external agencies. As discussed previously, the amount of time necessary to deal with these problems was a major reason for considering realignment. While the Liaison Committee has authority to act on minor issues that arise without further recourse to Joint Group approval, it is expected that major issues will be decided upon by the Joint Group. In such cases, the responsibility of the Liaison Committee will be

a) To clarify the specific issue and explore the implications of alternative decisions for presentation to the Joint Committee.

b) To call meetings of the Joint Group when the need arises, but at least once a year. Since one reason for realignment was to reduce the number of meetings that principals in particular were required to attend, Joint Group meetings should be held to a minimum. When the number of schools in the Project reaches a substantial level, it may be possible, with administrative consent, to combine such occasional meetings with county-wide meetings of principals (these are already held at regular intervals). This arrangement would have the dual advantage of reducing the gross number of meetings that Project members must attend and disseminating information about the Project to non-Project members. Through listening to discussions of current issues, these nonmembers would be given a reasonably accurate notion of what participation in the Project implied.

c) To further define their own role, subject to the agreement of the Joint Group. Since the inception of the Project and through all the stages outlined in figure 1, the county boards of education have been invited to send representatives to all meetings. This practice will continue, with one public school superintendent and one separate school superintendent acting in an advisory capacity to the Liaison Committee.

COMMUNICATION NETWORK

The communication chart shown in figure 2 indicates the main communication links among the Project elements. For the first element, the student, the communication links are unchanged as a result of the diffusion activities, but interaction with parents and teacher on a one-to-one basis may be more frequent than before. The teacher has no new basic communication links as a result of the diffusion activity, except insofar as he is involved in training programs undertaken by OISE personnel or other outsiders. In this case, he chooses to receive the instruction, and does so with the full endorsement of and in liaison with his principal. The new tasks that the teacher takes on as a result of the diffusion are essentially planning activities. These follow the more or less standard pattern of attention to goals, specification of goals, isolation of problems, ordering of problems in priority categories, search for solutions, selection of solutions, and implementation of solutions. Since most of these planning activities are undertaken in school time, the overall work load of the teacher should be not increased but rather rearranged to permit more planning time. In addition to the planning tasks, the teacher has training tasks, evaluation tasks, and more planning in his new role within the diffusion model.

The parent has no new communication links as a result of the diffusion activities, but the nature of his communication and the variety of tasks he performs are new. In the first place, he is involved to a greater extent in the reviewing of goals for the community school through participation in public meetings at the school level. Another set of new tasks emerges as the parent becomes a volunteer aide to the

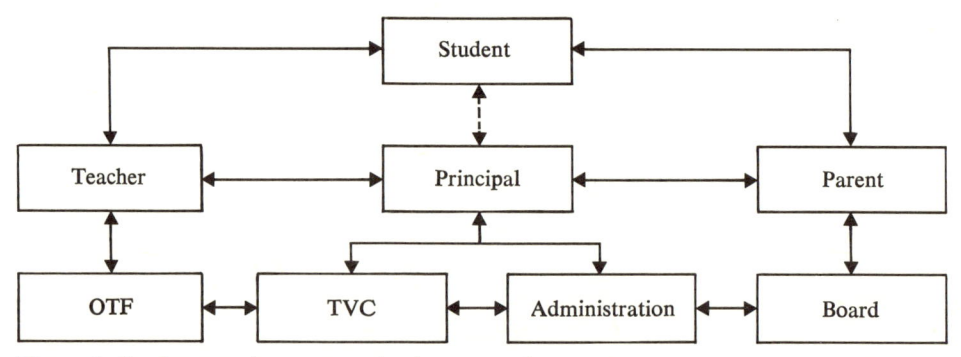

Figure 2. Implementation communication network.

schools and participates in a broad array of classroom activities, extending from full instruction of a large group to direct discussion with the individual student and the marking of his written work.

The principal has some new communication links that result from the diffusion activities. First, he communicates with the TVC. Second, he communicates with other principals in the Project groups. This latter link is not specifically shown in figure 2, but it is implicit throughout the program. At the task level, the principal is responsible for generating horizontal communication links among the teachers on his staff, and between his staff and the staff of other cooperating schools. He is responsible in all phases of diffusion for the progress of students in his school, and hence he is responsible at each stage of diffusion both for the initial activities associated with the Core Group or Study Group and for the final adoption activities undertaken on his behalf by his staff. As the central communicator in the system, the principal is responsible for all the vital communication links that must be established and maintained for realization of the system's potential.

The administration group of the board of education has a new communication link to contend with between the TVC and its own group. In the case of Peterborough County, this link was initiated at the county level and enthusiastically supported and maintained at the OISE–TVC level. In other counties of Region 9, the initial communication has been established, but plans to implement a full-scale diffusion activity are still tentative.

The communication network established in figure 2 emphasizes the strong role that must be taken by the school principal, and it supports the concept of the school as the basic unit in education. An unwilling or reluctant principal can destroy or minimize the impact of the system, but as the system is designed, there are reasonable incentives for the principal to participate. One important incentive is the central role played by him – a role that is willingly assumed by most principals. A second incentive is the basic wish to make educational progress in an empirically testable way. The system's negative features, from the point of view of some principals, include the problems of accommodating to variation in wishes of parents and variation in wishes of staff members. Also, there is the problem of relying on the judgment of staff members even when this conflicts with the judgment of the principal himself.

The chief education officer for both the public schools and the separate schools is the director of education. He is supported by superintendents who are responsible for geographical areas of the jurisdiction, and it is these superintendents who work closely with the principals and the TVC, with the full endorsement of the directors. The support of the superintendent groups has made possible the assignment of experienced teachers to the Core and Study Group schools where implementation or trial adoption of an innovation is planned; furthermore, through the cooperation of the superintendents, transfers of principals required by events external to the diffusion system have been arranged to serve the diffusion system, or to avoid interference with it. Transfers of both staff and principals within the school system seem to foster the spread of innovative ideas and in general represent a positive force in the diffusion program.

Some changes have taken place in the relationships between the TVC and external agencies that have been drawn into the diffusion activities. In the case of the local teachers' college, the first attempt to utilize students was particularly successful. It depended on the selection of forty-five of the best students from the college and their assignment to Project schools for half-day periods during the latter half of the first year of operation. In an attempt to expand the number of teachers' college students who would profit by experience in the Project, and to increase the number of schools that could profit by such an infusion of manpower, a volunteer system of participation was organized during the second year that potentially would yield up to a hundred students for half-day periods, for fifteen to twenty days per year.

There are many problems with the volunteer system, the most serious of which is the lack of commitment on the part of some volunteers to abide by their agreement. In addition, some school staff tend to assign the volunteer labor to menial clerical tasks that they themselves wish to avoid. At present, a modified volunteer system is yielding fewer teachers' college students, but the success of the program seems to be increasing.

Students from the local college of applied arts and technology have been used either on a voluntary basis or on a course program basis. This source of manpower may not have been fully exploited to date, but it appears that there is considerable success in its use so far.

University psychology students have emerged as yet another group of volunteers. As part of their regular program of studies, these students are required to prepare term papers that depend upon their work in the schools, and the arrangement seems a satisfactory one.

CHARACTERISTICS OF INNOVATIONS UNDER CONSIDERATION

The major innovations that the Study Group is considering are IPI, Conceptual Skills, School C Mathematics, School A Social Studies, Junior Language Laboratories, OTF Science, AAAS Science, and Tannenbaum Science. The first four of these programs are discussed in detail in chapters 5 and 7. IPI is a response to the need for individual pacing of student progress. Conceptual Skills is designed to remedy the problems of inadequate preparation in kindergarten for the conceptual program of grade 1. The School C Mathematics Program is a local attempt to individualize and vitalize junior mathematics. Similarly, the other innovations have specific purposes. Each innovation that is currently under trial adoption is considered by the staff to be a reasonable alternative to the existing program and an alternative that is potentially more powerful.

IPI requires a total reorganization of the mathematics program within classes, and it is greatly dependent upon the assistance of teacher aides. The School C program depends on organization across classes, as well as on some reorganization within classes. Conceptual Skills requires virtually no reorganization, but it does depend on a highly structured presentation to the total group or to a large group within a kindergarten class for approximately twenty-five minutes per day.

OUTSIDE THE PROJECT COUNTY The groundwork has been laid in two other counties for the introduction of a similar innovative program. In one county, the Conceptual Skills Program is the central item in a general trend toward innovation; and although a diffusion model has not been formally adopted by the administration, the idea has been presented and apparently well received.

In the other county, one principal has already attended a sufficient number of Core and Study Group meetings to permit his use as a central resource person in the establishment of a core group in the area. Whether or not a core group will emerge and, if so, when this will happen are not yet clear. One high-school principal, however, has expressed a desire to begin work in the area of mathematics as a cooperative venture with his feeder schools. Should this desire come to fruition, these schools will themselves provide a nucleus from which the Project can spread.

The head of the TVC has met with most of the public- and separate-school directors of education within Region 9. In each case, the visit to the local administration offices was initiated by the director of education. The directors who have not yet responded will be given further indications of the TVC's willingness to plan such a visit and to discuss possible liaison.

The TVC liaison with the Region 9 office of the Ministry of Education was established early through a visit by Field Development Central Staff officials and the TVC head to the Region 9 Head Office. Subsequent visits by the TVC's staff to the Region 9 office and visits of the Region 9 personnel to the TVC number more than twenty, and the frequency of visits is increasing as the consultant staff find they are welcome in the Centre.

One possible outcome of the liaison activities between the TVC and the departmental consultants is an increased interest on the part of the consultants in domain-referenced testing, and in particular in the domain-referenced or criterion-referenced testing associated with the innovations within the Project. The mathematics consultant in Region 9 has become sufficiently interested in both the criterion-referenced testing of the TVC and the two innovative mathematics programs within the Project that he has nominated people to work with the project director and has worked with her himself on the Evaluation Materials Package for grades 4, 5, and 6 mathematics. This package is essentially a repository of objectives and test items covering the full range of topics taught across the province. In effect, such liaison means that throughout Region 9 teachers can be made aware of the mathematics innovations within the Project through communication with their departmental consultant, and can profit by the evaluation data already available and the evaluation procedures outlined for use in individual schools.

In the event that other objectives pools and evaluation materials packages can be initiated in other subject fields, and in the event that there is departmental endorsement by the consultants of such activities, the stage will be set for a departmental takeover of the kind of diffusion activities initiated by the Project. This seems to be clearly in the best interests of the TVC, in view of the diminishing need for research and development as the diffusion model stabilizes and the processes become more clearly defined.

CONCLUSION The process variables discussed in this chapter are necessary for the creation or adoption of educational programs that represent a change in a demonstrably positive direction from the prior program. They are consistent with objectives endorsed by teachers as appropriate for their students. The requirement that there be an end product and that this product change student behavior means that Project members must acquire skills and strategies for curriculum development. It also means that evaluation must play a central role in any strategy for such curriculum development. The development of Project curricula is the subject of the next chapter.

CHAPTER 5

Development of innovative programs

The previous chapter described in some detail the process of diffusion as it has occurred and is occurring in the Project. The referent of this diffusion process has so far been itself a process – the process of teacher planning and reallocation of responsibility for educational change and innovation. It is tempting to consider these process components as ends in themselves, to be judged largely on the basis of their internal, logical consistency, their intuitive appeal, or both. Such a method of assessment, however, would be analogous to judging a teacher's effectiveness by observing only his behavior in the classroom (as is typically the case) and not the change in the behavior of students that is attributable to his behavior. Obviously, many instructional means or types of teacher behavior are effective in producing a given instructional end. It would be equally illogical to accept the value of the change process described here without some systematic evaluation of the end product of that process. Such evaluative data are the criteria by which the utility of the means (process) can be determined.

The end product of this process of change is change in student behavior – change in student behavior of a demonstrably different sort or greater amount than would have occurred had the process not been effected. The end product to be used as the major evaluative criteria is not, ultimately, happier teachers, better-informed parents, different curricula, or innovative classroom organization and teaching techniques, although some of these changes probably will occur. These results are, in fact, part of the process (secondary data) and as such need to be described if we are to understand fully the means used to achieve the end, the differential change in student behavior.

In this chapter, we will describe the most powerful components of change over which the schools have control – curricula. Curricula included in the Project are of two sorts. The first constitute well-developed, imported curricular packages (such as IPI mathematics and the Conceptual Skills Program) that are felt by teachers to meet high priority needs of their students better than existing programs do. Such programs are obviously worth serious consideration when change is contemplated, since the resources expended on their development far surpass those available to any school unit. A second and more common type of program has resulted from efforts by local teachers to meet educational objectives identified as important, but neither included in developed curricular packages nor satisfactorily achieved by their present curriculum.

LOCAL CURRICULUM DEVELOPMENT

During the school year of 1970/71, there were two locally developed programs in the Project for which data have been collected – a mathematics program and a social studies program, both designed for the junior elementary grades. In addition, at least five others have been put in a form which can be implemented in the classroom shortly and for which data have been gathered in the 1971/72 school year. These include two programs in reading, two in language arts, and one in mathematics. The task of devising such programs is substantial for teachers, and a method for doing so merits some discussion. While the following strategy has certainly not been followed explicitly by all teacher groups building curricula themselves, the components are implied in all their work and have been followed explicitly in three instances, largely as a result of consultation with the TVC. The elements of this strategy are illustrated in figure 3.

The major components of this strategy include educational objectives toward which the curriculum is directed (1 and 2), the means whereby these objectives are achieved (3), and the techniques used to determine the extent to which the purposes of the curriculum are achieved (4). Logically, the first three of these components are undertaken in the order illustrated; the evaluation component intervenes in all four stages. From a psychological or practical viewpoint, various teacher groups have found appropriate starting points and have proceeded, from the logical point of view, both backward and forward to complete the task. Several groups, for example, have begun with a vague notion of their purpose (1), moved next to an examination of materials associated with that purpose (3), only to realize that they must determine much more precisely what it is that they are trying to do (2) in order to discriminate rationally among available methods and materials (4). Similarly, it could be extremely profitable for a group of teachers to begin with a decision to evaluate their present program (4) that would necessitate further thought about present objectives (1 and 2). Before items were generated to test objectives, some new objectives probably would be added and old ones deleted. Along with at least minor revision of methods and materials (3), the program eventually evaluated (4) probably would not be the one originally subjected to scrutiny.

EDUCATIONAL OBJECTIVES Educational objectives that are of most value to the curriculum-building process are stated in terms of the observable performance of the student upon completion of some portion of instruction. These student performance objectives have two central functions. One function is to enable the teacher to communicate — communicate to himself about instructional goals and thereby design appropriate learning experiences, communicate to students about his expectations, and communicate to others in the instructional milieu (teachers and principals). The other function is the development of test items. If these functions are to be performed adequately, there must be a statement of objectives describing how the learner will demonstrate his attainment of the objective, describing the conditions (if any) under which the learner

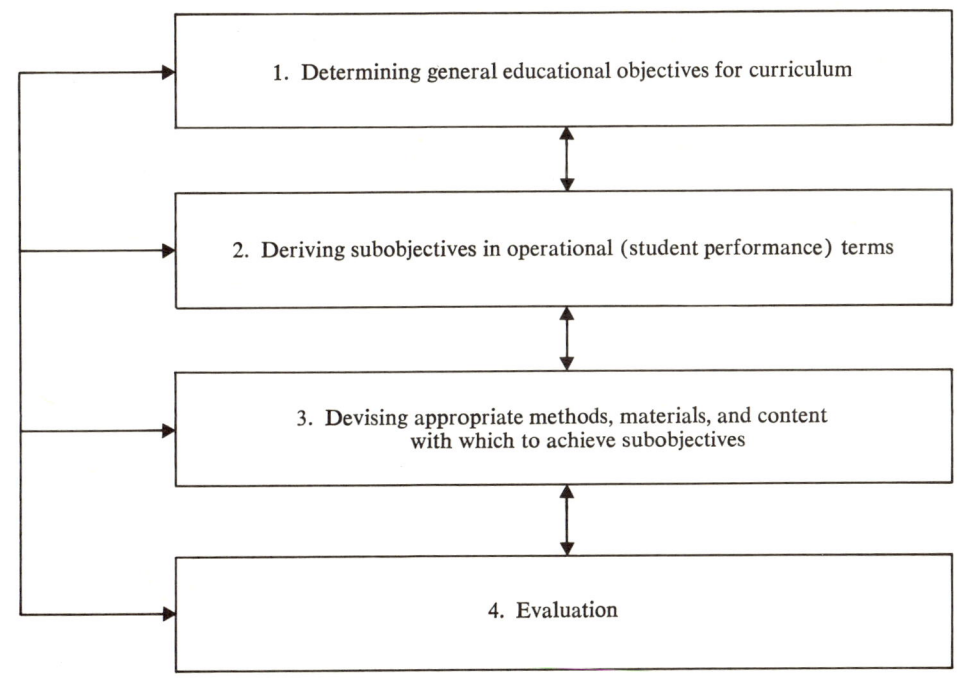

1. Determining general educational objectives for curriculum

2. Deriving subobjectives in operational (student performance) terms

3. Devising appropriate methods, materials, and content with which to achieve subobjectives

4. Evaluation

Figure 3. A strategy used by teachers in developing curriculum.

demonstrates his competence, and stating the standard of performance expected of the learner (Mager, 1962). Care must be taken to specify standards that are meaningful and that fall within the range of abilities of the target population (Garvin, 1970). An example of a mathematics student performance objective meeting these criteria is the following: Given the problem, paper, pencil, and two minutes (conditions), the student must be able to multiply any three-digit number by any two-digit number (learner action) correctly 90 percent of the time (standards).

As this objective suggests, although it often may be difficult to specify the conditions and standards of an objective (Melching, 1966), by far the greatest problem for teachers building curricula relates to the number of objectives that require attention in any proposed program. The IPI mathematics program, for example, is designed to achieve 390 separate student performance objectives. Clearly, the task is a long-term one, requiring a strategy that will assist in both determining an initiation point and providing mechanisms for work to be cumulative over long periods of time. One possible strategy involves a number of steps that are designed to be followed sequentially, but may be reordered as psychological or practical considerations dictate. These steps include:

1. Devising a comprehensive list of general objectives
2. Hierarchical ordering of general objectives
3. Determining available resources
4. Deciding on an initial general objective and developing related lower-level objectives

Performance objectives may be usefully stated at three levels of specificity that Ammerman (1966) labels *general*, *terminal*, and *enabling*. The first step in this sequence requires making explicit all the general objectives (for example, the learner is able to comprehend written English) that the proposed curriculum might have. Limited resources usually dictate that the short-term goal of the curriculum developer is to focus on only one of these general objectives, although the long-term goal may well be to work progressively toward comprehensive curriculum development. This requires an overview of the total task as a means of determining the most appropriate general objective with which to begin. Two important criteria employed in selecting general objectives include achievability and desirability, or what Pratt (1971) calls significance, both relative and absolute. A decision as to whether a given general objective is achievable within a given curriculum necessitates finding a basis in the curriculum for expecting that it is. That basis may depend in part on whether the behavior associated with the objective would be modifiable primarily within the curriculum or apart from, or in spite of, school activity (Dressel, 1960).

After a comprehensive list of achievable, desirable general objectives has been developed (this may be very short if generality is extreme), the objectives must be ranked. The two sets of criteria appropriately applied at this point may, in fact, produce two hierarchies of the same objectives. The first ranking may be according to the relative importance or functionality of the objective in the judgment of the curriculum developers (Pratt, 1971) – a judgment based on student, community, and larger social needs, as well as on specificity. Often, the more specific a given general objective is to a subject area, the greater priority it should be awarded. In a hierarchy of objectives associated with physical and health education, the objective of demonstrating good citizenship may be considered of lower priority than increased skill in performance of gross motor tasks, since the former objective, unlike the latter, crosses many subject areas and is not likely to be absent from a student's total educational experience. Nevertheless, the hierarchy of general objectives thus formed may be idealistic in the sense that those objectives characteristically given highest priority are the most complex, abstract, and difficult to achieve and evaluate. It is necessary, therefore, to reconsider this list in the light of the criteria of simplicity, concreteness, and importance in curriculum content. These criteria, in combination with assessments of available resources (the major one in this Project being cooperative teacher planning time), enable the curriculum developer to choose an important general objective that can be competently developed into part of an instructional program.

After the initial general objective is determined, both terminal and enabling objectives must be identified before the associated learning experience can be planned. Terminal objectives specify meaningful units of performance having value in and of themselves; they establish the performance criteria to be attained at the end of instruction. Enabling objectives consist of intermediate components requiring learner mastery before attainment of the terminal objective is possible. It is important that enabling and terminal objectives be clearly distinguished, for statements of enabling objectives have focus and meaning only through their association with a terminal objective. Failure to understand this relationship leads to a discouraging proliferation of microscopic statements that makes it very difficult to organize and evaluate learning experiences.

Since these three categories of objectives represent points on a generality–specificity continuum, there will be patterns of outcome statements that do not readily fit such a threefold system. In these cases, it is possible to establish subcategories of enabling objectives. Further specificity in most cases, however, serves only to fracture the terminal objective beyond a point essential for either effective communication or the development of an efficient strategy for achieving that objective. The magnitude of the task involved in specifying student performance objectives and the obvious utility of criterion-referenced information for instruction (see chapter 6) suggest the need for a solution that will minimize the former and maximize the latter for teachers. One solution is the development of behavioral objectives item pools by subject-matter experts and professional objectives writers that are similar to the Instructional Objectives Exchange (Popham, 1971), but have the more desirable features of a project now under way at OISE directed by Dorothy Horn in the field of mathematics. Such pools typically consist of a comprehensive list of student performance objectives for a given subject area and a large number of items that can be used to test mastery of each objective. It seems reasonable to suggest that such pools may also be extended to act as a focus for the development of instructional materials and techniques appropriate to the development of specific objectives by educators and publishers of instructional materials.

A central file of such objectives, test items, and associated materials and techniques, located in teacher resource centers, would enable teachers to design programs of their own that combine the advantages of both packaged and locally designed curricula. Not only would each teacher be able to base selection decisions on an intimate knowledge of specific student needs, but the resultant process and product would have the same potential returns that are now available only from large-scale curriculum projects with the resources to employ the best technological and subject-matter experts in their development.

PROJECT CURRICULA AND SCHOOLS

As time has elapsed, and as some of the main strengths and weaknesses of the Project have become evident, it has been necessary to make changes at both the school level and the program level. The major strength of the Project – the need for regularly scheduled meetings during which teachers can discuss together the program that is implemented in their school – is also its weakness. While the planning activity is central to the generation of a climate for change, arranging for planning time threatens to destroy the calm of this desirable climate. A second feature that appears to be a weakness of the Project concerns the orientation of new personnel to the philosophy and mechanics of the program. Ultimately, this shifting of personnel may become a positive feature, since teachers who have been moved out of one participating school become change leaders in newly organized schools. The third problem, that again is a felt need of the teachers, is the acquisition of current information about innovative projects in other Core schools, as well as innovative projects around the county and beyond; but although teachers feel that this is a problem, they recognize that the relationship to the TVC program is of considerable help.

School A

The staff of Public School A at the junior-division level have introduced their own thematic approach in social studies. The sociological study by McGill and Skinner (1970) describes many of the classroom activities considered important in the school setting. There is clear evidence of positive attitudes on the part of teachers and their general acceptance of new roles involving responsibility for program development. A second study at this school has been conducted by the principal in cooperation with the TVC (Montgomery, 1970). In this thorough report, the focus is on student attitudes, and it generally concludes that students have a highly favorable response to the program introduced in their school. A further analysis of attitude toward a number of the features of the thematic-based program shows a positive acceptance and feeling of satisfaction as to the amount of learning that has taken place. Although the curriculum development strategy outlined earlier was not followed initially, a later request for evaluation has led to the cooperative generation of sixty student performance objectives common to the "research skills" section of the grades 4, 5, and 6 social studies program. Test items subsequently have been written for each of these objectives. (The results of the assessment of this portion of the program are given in chapter 7.) At the time of writing, requests have been made by the teachers for consultation regarding objectives and item revision. This activity has been projected for 1971/72, as well as possible evaluation of other components of the social studies program.

Partly as a result of the efforts of the junior-grade staff in connection with this program, the intermediate teachers at the school have initiated a program of their own in basic reading skills. They have developed a climate for change and are presently working on objectives, materials, and diagnosis in the area of reading comprehension, following very precisely the strategy outlined earlier.

Besides the social studies program at the junior-grade level and the reading work at the intermediate level, the staff have introduced Conceptual Skills at the K–1 level as well as innovations of their own in connection with the volunteer assistants from various community and academic areas.

School B

The feature effort of the staff at School B has been the introduction of Individually Prescribed Instruction (IPI) during the 1970/71 school year. This particular program component is common to both School B and School E, and its description is provided elsewhere (see chapter 7). Besides the IPI program, School B's staff have produced some other innovations originating within the school. One component involves social studies at the grade 6 level. Another is OTF Science in cooperation with the TVC and the field officer for the OTF Science Program. Another component involves language arts with the assistance of a faculty member of the local teachers' college.

School C

A teacher-built mathematics program has been the main thrust of the staff of School C since it entered the Project during 1968/69. In this school, the climate for change or self-renewal has led the staff to develop virtually on their own a total mathematics program for the junior division that is basically individualized.

The purposes and performance objectives of the math program are essentially the same now as they were when it was first started. There are, however, process revisions as well as revisions and adaptations within the instructional framework. One major process change concerns the grouping of students. Early reports indicated that cross-grade groups operated effectively as a means of increasing the amount of individualization available to students. Experience with this innovative process has led the teachers to reverse their earlier decisions and retain the regular class groupings. The general staff view is that teachers profit more by knowing their students well than they do by knowing the particular sections of work and by having a relatively homogeneous group of students to deal with. Furthermore, they feel that record-keeping or tracking of student progress is more readily handled within class groups than on a broader basis when the teacher sees a greater number of students.

During 1970/71, in consultation with the TVC, criterion-referenced test items for each of the math program objectives were written at each of the grades 4, 5, and 6 levels. The pretests were used by the teachers as diagnostic instruments, and when they were combined with the posttest, a gain score could be derived that assessed the curriculum in terms of student achievement. As with the social studies program of School A, a form for recording test results that maximized their diagnostic value was created.

It is important to note that teachers, students, and parents accurately interpret achievement tests in norm-referenced terms because of past familiarity. The communication of the same test results in criterion-referenced terms, however, requires a much different interpretive framework and report form. In particular, students and parents need to be made aware of the two uses of the achievement test designed as a domain-referenced or criterion-referenced instrument. When administered prior to instruction, the criterion-referenced measure is diagnostic (Ward, 1970), since it precisely identifies the initial relevant competencies of the learner entering the instructional milieu. As Glaser (1967) states: "Without the assessment of initial learner characteristics, carrying out an educational procedure is a presumption. It is like prescribing medication for an illness without first describing the symptoms [p. 6]."

Such measurement enables the instructor to work with the student specifically in the areas of his demonstrated weaknesses and to avoid wasting resources on unnecessary instruction. Because this assessment is in terms of post-instructional student performance objectives, however, it is particularly susceptible to misinterpretation. Considerable care must be taken in specifying to both students and parents that pretests are for the purpose of identifying weaknesses and that low scores therefore should be expected.

When instruction is preceded by a diagnostic test and followed by a posttest, student achievement can be reported as a "change score" (posttest score minus pretest score). In terms of criterion testing, the point that must be made explicit is that the magnitude of this change score, across all students exposed to the instructional treatment, is primarily an index of treatment efficiency and secondarily an index of student ability. Small change scores across groups, then, indicate curriculum revision, not student failure.

The results of criterion-referenced measurement can be reported either as specific information or as a score (Lindvall & Nitko, 1969). Criterion-referenced information is available whenever student performance objectives have been stated and test items developed to assess each objective. Results can be examined in as detailed a fashion as necessary to gain the required information. For example, a checklist may be derived indicating that the child has or has not achieved a given objective. Although checklists are often used in primary education, it is usually necessary to state explicitly the standards required for achievement. Because such reporting is cumbersome if applied on a wide scale, some attempts have been made to use a score. The nature of criterion-referenced measures dictates, however, that the score also describe precisely achievement of specific educational objectives. Since on most tests the same score can be obtained through many different response patterns, this criterion is not easily met. In order to streamline reporting by the use of scores, it is necessary to be satisfied with less specific information or to develop sequentially scaled tests (Guttman, 1944; Lindvall & Nitko, 1969; Popham & Husek, 1969; Cox & Graham, 1966). A sequentially scaled test is one that empirically demonstrates a hierarchical dependency among objectives – that is, the achievement of one objective depends on achieving a lower-level objective, and any given score from such a test describes an invariable response pattern. Although it is possible to devise such tests (Cox & Graham, 1966), the probability of doing so in most content areas is very low. While there may appear to be a logical conceptual dependency, it is unlikely that an empirical dependency can be demonstrated. The most useful reporting form seems to be one that lies between the checklist of enabling objectives and a single score, probably centering around multiple scores reflecting the achievement of terminal objectives.

As School C's math program has become more refined, the amount of materials for instruction and record-keeping has increased greatly. It is significant that this array of materials includes some commercially available packages for short-term use; in some instances, these consist of cards, tapes, and worksheets.

The use of parent volunteers has been a major feature of the program since the early days of the Project. In 1970/71, the school was a focus of attention for a research study on the use of parent volunteers under the direction of an academic staff member from the Office of Field Development at OISE. Some of the features of the parental involvement at School C are unique to the school program, and many more have been pioneered at the Niagara Centre (OISE).[1] Descriptive data, evaluative data, and a thorough review of the related literature on parental involvement are now in preparation. The School C staff also are involved in innovative programs beyond their mathematics program and parental involvement. Conceptual Skills, OTF Science, Inquiry Training, and reading are in various stages of field testing.

School D
This school encountered a unique situation among Project schools during the 1970/71 school year. The principal, vice-principal, and three of the five original Project teachers became dissociated from the staff and hence much of the work of creating a climate for change had to be repeated. It is perhaps important to report that the principal at School D during 1969/70 did not hold a permanent appointment. During that period and as of the 1970/71 school year, he had a permanent appointment as a school principal in a smaller school that is presently associated with the Study Group. The vice-principal from School D during the 1969/70 school year became a project officer with the Trent Valley Centre. Furthermore, one of the teachers who left School D was transferred to another Project school and another teacher returned to full-time studies at university. But what began as almost an entirely new Core school in September 1970 has emerged as a full-fledged Core school. Not only has it implemented the Conceptual Skills Program and parts of the OTF Science Program, but it is embarking on its own unique school program in the area of language arts. Early descriptions of the program indicate that some prelimi-

---

[1]These have been described in Brison, Hedges, and Robinson (1970).

nary work was done in the area of social studies; because of the high rate of turnover of staff and the slightly different tastes of the newly appointed staff, however, the general direction of the new program is somewhat different than it was in 1969/70. Along with the concentration on language arts, the staff have given special attention to the Imperial Reading Lab and the Controlled Reader, both of which are available within the school. The group planning sessions seem to be used to discuss ways of making efficient use of these two packaged program components, and there is also considerable planning concerning unique features of the language program for the specific use of students in School D. The social studies program developed prior to 1970/71 has not been dropped entirely. In fact, the two remaining staff members from the 1969/70 group not only have continued to use the program, but have developed it further and are promoting its use with at least two of the remaining four teachers who have shown some willingness to try it.

School E
This school program was enhanced by the introduction of Individually Prescribed Instruction throughout grades 4, 5, and 6 during 1970/71. Although the efforts required to sustain IPI have introduced considerable strain on manpower planning, a number of less visible changes also have been introduced. These include a regular daily assembly, an increased number of subject-integrated field trips, the use of community personnel as resource persons, and increased small-group and individual instruction, as well as considerable student freedom in the choice of some tasks and the means of achieving them. A systematic revision of some aspects of the social science program has also begun.

INDIVIDUALLY PRESCRIBED INSTRUCTION (MATHEMATICS) Two of the Core schools used a packaged mathematics program called Individually Prescribed Instruction for the junior grades during the 1970/71 school year. The materials, training, testing, and general classroom management are common to schools B and E, but the total mathematics program for each school is not the same. School E, for example, uses IPI only four of the five days per week; the work during the fifth day varies from problem-solving to remedial activities through instruction in regular math topics. School B's staff also supplement the IPI materials in their math program, but they are organized differently to do it.

The IPI mathematics program was developed by Research for Better Schools, Inc., part of the University of Pittsburgh's Learning Research and Development Center. The program consists of 390 sequenced student performance objectives, programmed materials to be used by students in achieving the objectives, and test items to assess mastery of objectives. Each of the objectives fits into one of thirteen arithmetic skill areas, and each area consists of levels A to I, corresponding roughly to grade levels. The thirteen skill areas comprise numeration, place value, addition, subtraction, multiplication, division, combination of processes, fractions, money, time, systems of measurement, geometry, and special topics. The primary purpose of the program is individualization of student instruction in terms of both rate and content exposure. Each student is theoretically able to work as fast as he wishes, and also is exposed to only as much of the programmed content as is necessary to achieve a given objective. The latter feature, in particular, is ensured through a precise system of pupil achievement diagnosis and subsequent prescription writing. With this system, the student is given a placement test that approximately determines his level of competence for each skill area when he enters the program. Then he is pretested to diagnose his specific competencies at his placement level, and a prescription of work is written for him by the teacher that he is expected to be able to complete largely by himself with the self-instructional material. Curriculum-embedded tests and posttests are later given to assess his mastery of specific objectives and levels so that further work can be prescribed by the teacher.

The task of the teacher using this program is mainly to write prescriptions for his students based on test results and on his knowledge of the students' abilities. The tests are marked by teacher aides who work both in and out of the classroom — sometimes in the paper materials room, where they also assist students in finding prescribed materials, although this is a task that most perform independently. The records of student progress are kept in individual student files, and each student has a Student Record Profile that shows at a glance his progress in all thirteen skill areas.

The Project schools that have selected IPI are probably different from most IPI schools in that they have first specified the goals of their program and later found that their goals for students are very similar or almost identical to the goals of the IPI program. Having recognized this similarity, the teachers have found it easier to identify with the program than might otherwise have been possible. They understand the role of performance objectives, and they are fully aware of the diagnostic capabilities of the pretests, curriculum-embedded items, and posttests.

The daily routine in IPI is considerably different from the daily routine in a typical class setting, but again the teachers already have modified their daily routine as a result of their involvement in the Project. Consequently, the change to an IPI routine is not a great burden.

One of the first questions asked by the teachers and later by the parents is "What do you do about students who get much further ahead than their classmates or much further behind?" Also, "What do you do at the end of the grade 6 year when the students may be scattered over several grades?" These questions have plagued IPI schools and most other schools that have dealt with students as individuals since the beginning of education as a formal activity. Most teachers and many parents realize that the grade system, with its appearance of uniform progress, has not really yielded uniform progress at all; in fact, the spread of youngsters over a continuum of achievement levels may be as great in the grade system as it is within the individualized system. The fact that teachers no longer worry about these particular questions and that parents have become less concerned about them seems to be a healthy development.

The one major problem with IPI that is as yet unresolved is its present cost ($12 per student). Clearly, this sum is too high for most schools, and yet there is the possibility and indeed the probability that the gains resulting from the program will be sufficient to warrant a careful study of costs and benefits. If the preliminary assessment by classroom teachers is any indication of the ultimate assessment of student progress, there are indeed considerable benefits from using the IPI program.

CONCEPTUAL SKILLS PROGRAM The Bereiter–Regan program entitled Conceptual Skills was introduced in five Project schools during 1970/71, and in two schools beyond this group. The program has been described by Regan (1970), and an evaluation of its early introduction in the Metropolitan Toronto area has been prepared by Scardemalia and Bereiter (1971).

The planning for the introduction of the Conceptual Skills Program in the Core schools began in the fall of 1969, when one or two Core principals became interested in what they heard about the program at North Bridlewood, in Scarborough. After a preliminary visit to that school and to a school where the program was just beginning, a group of principals and kindergarten teachers made further observations of the program and engaged in a lengthy discussion of its merits with program representatives. A training program was then provided for those teachers who had agreed with their principal in wanting to go ahead with the program.

There seem to be strong indications that teachers are well satisfied with the program, which requires approximately 25 to 30 minutes per day of instruction time. Although the materials embody a rigid conceptual structure that is presented in sequence, there is no reason for the teacher to alter his instructional style; and there is no reason for the remaining part of the day, beyond the 25 minutes, to be in any way different from what it would be in the absence of the Conceptual Skills Program.

OTF SCIENCE PROGRAM Each of the Core schools has implemented in some form a portion of the OTF Science Program that is characteristically presented by an OTF science consultant in a series of teacher workshops. The feature of the Core schools' operation that sets them apart from other schools that are implementing the OTF Science Program is the availability of the consultant for intensive classroom observation and participation. While most schools rely on the consultant's presentations at workshops to ensure the integrity of the program, the Core schools have acquired his services through the TVC for approximately four days in each school. The extent to which this procedure enhances the value of the OTF Science Program is not clear, but there is some hope that it is substantial.

OTHER COMMON COMPONENTS Other components of the school program are used in more than one of the schools. At present, no specific evaluation activity is focused on any of these components; but as the preliminary trials give indications as to the merits of the program, there is an increased likelihood that more formal evaluation activities will be used. Formal evaluation tends to be more likely for those program components that have arisen through the participation of the TVC in the scanning and selection process. Also, evaluation is more likely for packaged materials that possess readily usable evaluation instruments. There will surely be some program components, however, that are worthy of formal assessment, even though the assessment interests and instruments must be developed from the beginning.

CHAPTER 6

The role of evaluation in school change: theoretical considerations

GOAL OF EVALUATION

Scriven (1967) has pointed to the distinction between the goals and roles of evaluation. He suggests there is a single goal – to make a judgment. Certain types of questions about certain entities must be answered in order to make possible an estimation of the merit, worth, or value of those entities.

This judgmental goal of evaluation is, according to Scriven, what educators want and hence should receive. Stake (1967) points out, however, that evaluation activity is frequently viewed as highly threatening to educators and that greater emphasis on its judgmental role will only increase their defensiveness and resistance to its use. He suggests that description is a second legitimate goal for evaluation that carries less negative affect.

But description is the essential means when gathering data to be used in making decisions, and judgment is the sole legitimate end of evaluation. The important issue here is the identity of the judge. This identity will largely determine the form (but probably not the nature) of the descriptive, evaluative data. We disagree with Scriven (1967) that the evaluator should be the judge and in this Project place the burden of judgment on the local educator (although he may, understandably, require assistance with interpretation).

Our rejection of the notion of evaluator-as-judge is based on the role of evaluation in the Project. Evaluation data are put to many uses – appraising individual student achievement, selecting students for courses or positions in short supply, diagnosing learning difficulties, program evaluation, national assessments of educational progress of large populations (Tyler, 1966), and others. These many uses or roles have been categorized, in a widely accepted manner, as being either formative or summative (Scriven, 1967): formative evaluation being designed to discover deficiencies and successes in the intermediate versions of new curricula, and summative evaluation relating primarily to adoption–rejection decisions. Unfortunately, as Madaus (1970) states, Scriven's dichotomous categorization has erroneously been taken to imply a difference in kind, when what exists is a difference in emphasis. The formative–summative distinction is irrelevant (Stake, 1969) to the choice of an evaluation strategy. It is probably more accurate to discuss formative and summative *uses of data* than formative and summative *types of evaluation*. In the Project, this distinction has resulted, not in the collection of different kinds of data, but in the reporting of data in different forms and at different frequencies. When formative information is appropriate, for example, data are reported to the teacher curriculum developers as they are collected and in a form usable for detailed curriculum revision. This applies to data collected by the TVC as well as data to which the Centre has immediate access as a result of its central position in the curriculum development process. Mehlinger's (1970) point is too frequently ignored and applies especially well to this Project in reference to the locally devised programs: "Probably the most useful and simple formative evaluation practice is for developers to teach students who are using the experimental course [p. 6]."

FUNCTIONS OF EVALUATION

Evaluation, as discussed, has been cast in many roles, most of which imply the possibility of changing the subject of evaluation as a result of this process. Certainly, the goal of evaluation – judging – implies action as a result of and in the direction suggested by the judgment. The exceedingly powerful formative role of evaluation in school change and innovation has rarely been made explicit, however, or even formally recognized within the larger, systematic framework of educational innovation.

Evaluation, considered in relation to school change, has three functions: to promote, to facilitate, and to validate change. First, examination of the components of the framework for change presented here clearly indicates a heavy dependency upon many kinds of evaluative data for the promotion of change. Such data are instrumental in precipitating a climate for change among principals and senior administrators by suggesting to them general areas in the educational environment in need of improvement and by providing them with a basis for rational decision making about appropriate action. They may also precipitate a climate for change among teachers and a commitment to action because of the concrete ways in which they can pinpoint high priority problem areas falling within the range of teacher responsibility.

Second, the uses of descriptive data in facilitating the implementation of change are readily apparent. The observations of classroom pupil behavior collected by

Yeager and Lindvall (1968), for example, provide Project teachers with a means of determining the adequacy of the behavior of their own students in the first year of IPI mathematics adoption. The same kind of assessment made of the Project classes in 1970/71 (reported in chapter 7) assists Project teachers in remedying areas of obvious weakness and provides other teachers in similar settings with a basis for formulating reasonable pupil behavior expectations should they adopt the program.

The third and perhaps most important function of evaluation is the validation of school change. Fullan, Eastabrook, and Hewson (1971) have noted that an assumption implicit in most research on school innovativeness is that specific innovations are good and valuable for the school to adopt. They suggest that this assumption is questionable on a number of grounds. First, the intrinsic quality of an innovation is often not the sole reason for its adoption. There may be many other reasons – the desire to be an early innovator, innovating for reward, and following administrative edict. Second, summative evaluation data may not be available for the innovation, often because it is falsely deemed unnecessary in the light of the favorable conditions of program development and expertise of the developers. Third, the aims of the new innovations are often so broadly and ambiguously stated that their assessment in an objective manner is extremely difficult. Fourth, even when data are available for summative purposes, schools differ sufficiently among themselves that decisions about the "extent of fit" between the innovation and the school are dependent upon further school-specific evaluation.

UTILITY AND FEASIBILITY OF OPERATIONAL OBJECTIVES

Evaluators have traditionally argued for the necessity of student performance objectives in order to operationalize an evaluation plan. Both the utility and feasibility of such performance objectives have been subject to varying degrees of criticism since their conception. The position taken by the evaluators of this Project as well as by others (for example, Popham, 1968), however, is that not only are student performance objectives indispensable and practical, particularly under the conditions of the Project, but they also have multiple payoffs, these payoffs relating directly to the promotion, facilitation, and validation functions of evaluation in school change.

Accountability and performance contracting, although unfamiliar to many educators a very short time ago, promise to be two of the most frequently printed terms in the educational literature of the 1970s.[1] The spirit of these two concepts, however, has been carefully built into our educational system since its inception.

[1]See, for example, Unfinished business in the teaching profession (1970).

Teachers have long been accountable to students, parents, and educational administrators for the performance of their students. Similarly, administrators are accountable to the public, through elected representatives on the boards of education, for the performance of those whom they administer. What is the reason, then, for the recent controversy over these issues?

The ceilings imposed by governments on educational spending across Canada and the United States demonstrate, in unmistakable terms, the public's disenchantment with the rationale for financing education over the past decade. Not only is it becoming increasingly difficult for the taxpayer to support rises in educational spending, but more critically, a law of diminishing returns appears to have been identified. These changes have resulted in considerable discussion about, if not real movement toward, a cost-benefit system of funding rarely imposed on the educational establishment of the past. Regardless of the specific outcome of this movement, it is reasonably certain that educators will feel obliged to demonstrate much more visibly and accurately than before the results of their intervention for both professional improvement and public accountability.

One of the oldest and potentially most effective means of increasing the visibility of educational intervention is through the specification of educational objectives in terms of learner outcomes (student performance objectives) amenable to relatively unambiguous evaluation. The clarity of communication, the resultant availability of data for diagnosis, evaluation, and display purposes, and the endorsed respectability of such objectives by the profession at large seem to provide sufficient impetus for their widespread use. This certainly has been the case with industries involved in educational performance contracting. It is not true, however, of the more traditional environments. Although many educators state objectives for their curricula, few do so in a manner that will satisfy questions about accountability. Objectives are typically stated at a level of generality that cannot lead directly to either classroom action or explication of the effect of that action.

Numerous reasons are given for failing to establish operationally specific objectives that provide a base for decision making about instructional materials and methodology and permit evaluation of pupil achievement in criterion-referenced terms. These fall into two main categories: first, reasons concerning the theoretical shortcomings of student performance objectives; and second, reasons concerning a number of practical problems, sometimes viewed as insurmountable, in achieving these objectives. The purpose of this discussion is to examine the magnitude of these apparent obstacles to the use of student performance objectives in evaluation and curriculum development, particularly since they potentially provide a partial solution to the accountability problem currently pressing on teachers.

THEORETICAL SHORTCOMINGS OF STUDENT PERFORMANCE OBJECTIVES

The major criticism leveled at the use of student performance objectives is based on an unwarranted and exclusive association of the use of such objectives with behaviorist learning theory and an unnecessarily limited view of the range of their application.

Those who object to the use of student performance objectives on theoretical grounds (for example, Ebel, 1967) suggest that, as educators, they are concerned with stimulating the development of complex cognitive structures, as opposed to the acquisition of specific knowledge. The former objective necessarily requires an extended period of time, while the latter may be acquired on a relatively short-term basis. It would be unrealistic, they argue, to expect to be able to observe results of intervention designed to stimulate the development of complex cognitive structures, schema, or images within as short a period of time as a semester or a school year, if in fact such results ever become directly observable. Student performance objectives are irrelevant under such conditions.

The acquisition of complex cognitive structures, however, is dependent upon the learner's making increasingly sophisticated hierarchical associations of specific content knowledge, or simpler, partially ordered construct components (Gagné, 1965; Miller, Galanter, & Pribram, 1960). These are in most cases subject to behavioral manifestation in the presence of an appropriate stimulus (a critical feature in relation to the pressure for public accountability). In consequence, the real issue here appears to be, not whether the learning of complex structures or specific knowledges is the primary cognitive objective of education — no one would seriously consider these as alternatives — but whether one should be concerned with systematically devising long-term patterns of intervention (means) whereby the development of complex cognitive structures (ends) may be stimulated in an ordered and efficient manner. If the educator accepts this responsibility in place of a more intuitive (sometimes called artistic) approach to instruction, he involves himself in (1) the specification of lower-level, observable, student performance structural components and (2) the assessment of component mastery as a diagnostic tool in the building of curricula designed to promote future mastery of complex cognitive structures. It is true that this approach carries with it the danger of losing sight of the relationship between the complex cognitive structure and the means devised to assist the learner in mastering this structure. Failure to recognize and avoid this pitfall may account for a large proportion of the misunderstanding alluded to above, as subobjectives designed as means become interpreted as ends to be justified in their own right. The same problem, however, is likely to occur with the intuitive approach, with the added disadvantage of uncertainty as to the logical relationship of chosen means to achieve specified ends.

A closely related criticism of student performance objectives relates to their limitations when general educational objectives are concerned with cognitive tools (styles, abilities), such as problem-solving strategies and perceptual acuity, rather than with conceptual structures embedded in a content domain. Here, it is suggested (Ebel, 1967), the emphasis should be on the cognitive input to decision making rather than the behavioral output, and student performance objectives are quite inappropriate for this purpose. There are two flaws in this argument. First, the activity of stating performance objectives does not mean that instructional emphasis is being put on behavioral output rather than cognitive input. It does suggest, however, that performance is the most visible manifestation of learning yet devised and, hence, the most objective way of evaluating and improving the effectiveness of the cognitive input. One might question the nature of cognitive input that does not result in some form of behavioral output. A second flaw in this argument involves the apparent assumption that cognitive tools are developed in abstract forms and then brought to bear on specific contents, when in fact the reverse is usually the case. Just as student performance objectives include both behavioral and content components, so cognitive tools typically develop in a context. If this context is sufficiently broad and properly introduced, limited transfer of strategies to similar problems in different contextual settings may occur. Nevertheless, with content added, behavior becomes potentially observable and student performance objectives are generally operable.

PROBLEMS IN OPERATIONALIZING STUDENT PERFORMANCE OBJECTIVES

Even if we assume there is agreement in theory with the purposes of student performance objectives, a number of problems remain that are believed to interfere with their operationalization. These problems can be broadly classified as having to do with timing their identification, optimizing their influence on curriculum development, and using them as a basis for curriculum evaluation.

We will deal with each of these problem areas in turn, but first we should note that these issues probably are not at the heart of the problem. In his well-known discussion of some of these pseudo issues, Eisner (1967) alludes to the central problem, although he fails to recognize it as such. He states that teachers do not seem to take educational objectives seriously, "*at least as they are prescribed from above*" (our emphasis), and then goes on to argue that if educational objectives are really useful tools, teachers will use them. If they do not, probably it is not that the teachers are at fault, but rather that the objectives are inappropriate or irrelevant. Evidence from this Project, one of the healthiest innovative school curriculum development projects in Ontario and possibly in Canada, strongly suggests that neither teachers nor the nature of objectives are to blame for the limited use made of objectives; rather, the fault lies in the "prescription from above" and the accountability to higher authority for achievement of these objectives.

Who chooses or designs the educational objectives is critical to the use made of them. It should be obvious by now that most curriculum innovation succeeds or fails on the basis of teacher acceptance of its validity and intent. It is equally evident that solutions to problems are utilized only by persons who recognize the problem as affecting them significantly. Educational objectives represent problems, and when these problems are identified by teachers as being critical to their functioning, solutions are sought and implementation is greatly stimulated. This is not to suggest that the process of transferring to teachers the responsibility for identifying educational objectives is an easy task, or even one that anyone knows very much about. It is, however, essential to the Project, and apparently it has enabled those involved to overcome, at least partially, the pseudo problems associated with specifying objectives. Teachers in the Project are continually building and revising curricula using this scientific or rational approach.

The major contribution of the Project lies in its diffusability and the generalizability of the diffusion model that is being developed. Because diffusion occurs at varying rates, the schools in the Project are at different, though overlapping, stages of the transfer process. Six stages can be identified, and an analysis of them provides an indication of how objectives are operationalized in the curriculum-building process.

Stage 1 in the Project is preceded by central administrative consent to autonomous school control by the principals, and consists of principals studying and talking among themselves about innovation and change. The principal plays the key role in the diffusion process, a much different role from his traditional one. He is both a precipitator and a facilitator of change. In the short run, he usually has to establish a general climate for change or dissatisfaction with the status quo among at least some members of his staff. A primary focus of discussion at stage 1, therefore, is the identification of techniques whereby this may be achieved.

Stage 2 involves trying out with the staff the techniques identified at stage 1 in an attempt to establish the climate for change. It should be noted here that although the principal may precipitate this climate, he makes every effort not to predetermine the specific educational objectives that may grow out of the change.[2] Critical to this and subsequent stages is the credibility with which the principal divests himself of decision-making authority in the curriculum area and deposits it with his staff. Many

---

[2]Sometimes, however, the principal may have to stimulate the staff by bringing a problem to their attention.

teachers seem willing to assume responsibility for curriculum development if they are first convinced that they are truly being entrusted with that responsibility. Teachers are, after all, usually considered most directly responsible for student performance; but in the past, they have not had sufficient control of curriculum to bear the accountability thus implied.

Stages 3 and 4 consist of identifying a problem usually common to two or more staff members at a relatively concrete level (such as a specific subject and grade) and a commitment by those staff members to work collectively toward a solution. As mentioned earlier, the logical counterpart of a problem is an objective – to find a solution. Inherent in these two stages, therefore, is the need to overcome some of the problems with operationalizing objectives and, particularly at these stages, those problems concerned with the timing of the identification of objectives.

Two obstacles have traditionally been associated with such timing. The first is the premise that educational objectives should be stated prior to the formulation of curriculum activities. While this is logically sound, it is probably not psychologically defensible. It has been pointed out that one can identify useful activities first and determine the objective of these activities later. This problem appears to resolve itself when it is teachers who determine objectives, since the first part of their task is to make explicit the objectives to which they implicitly adhere. To do this, they must look at their own activities – the choice of an activity presupposing a judgment as to the utility of that activity in achieving an objective, however well hidden and intuitively employed. Curriculum development at the teacher level therefore necessitates a constant interaction between objectives and activities, where both are employed dynamically to modify and expand one another through the process of formative evaluation.

The second problem in timing is the assumption that since many outcomes of instruction are not predictable before instruction, it is pointless to specify objectives prior to instruction. The fallacy of this reasoning is obvious. It should be noted, however, that because realistic objectives specified before instruction are more likely to receive instructional emphasis, criteria need to be established to screen the total complement of available objectives as a means of ensuring a workable number for both instruction and the diagnosis of learner weaknesses. This suggestion is in partial disagreement with Hastings (1967), who proposes that all outcomes should be amenable to the description specified. The cause of this discrepancy is that here teachers are advocated as the primary curriculum developers. Rarely does such a group have either the time or the need to deal comprehensively with all identifiable objectives in a content area beyond the general level. Part of their task, and one that only they can perform, is to select from the desirable general objectives those judged to be most important for their students and achievable with the resources indigenous to their schools.

The fifth and sixth stages of curriculum development in the Project focus on the discrimination of high priority general objectives and their subsequent operationalization. At these stages, the problems associated with optimizing the use of objectives and utilizing them for evaluation purposes are confronted. At stage 5, teachers must acquire curriculum development skills and increased content knowledge in the area chosen for examination. Here two problems concerned with optimization are evident. The first is determining the level of specificity at which objectives can be most usefully stated. Statements of objectives can be placed on a generality–specificity continuum, those lying at either of the extreme ends of the continuum being equally inoperable, although for different reasons. Very general statements obviously are too abstract to relate readily to classroom activity, while extremely specific objectives that proliferate in detail beyond a level required for reasonable communication lose their educational significance, thereby failing to generate appropriate activity. It is, nevertheless, necessary to begin with a general objective and determine lower-level objectives as antecedent conditions leading to its eventual achievement. Once again, the teacher is best qualified to determine the necessary level of specificity, using his knowledge of relevant student prerequisite mastery. For example, one group of intermediate-level elementary-school teachers in the Project that is working on a reading program has found Ammerman's (1966) tri-level specifications scheme useful, beginning with the general objective of increased reading comprehension.

The size of the task of specifying objectives in student performance terms should not be minimized. One group of teachers in the Project, focusing on a thematic social studies program, has spent approximately four months of weekly meetings in determining sixty student performance objectives and diagnostic test items for only the portion of that program labeled research skills. This does suggest an urgent need to search for means whereby the same point can be reached with less effort, while teacher-centered decision-making responsibility is still retained. One alternative that has been proposed (Leithwood, 1971) is the creation of objective and item pools generated by subject-matter experts in consultation with groups of teachers. The purpose of such pools is to provide teacher groups with a comprehensive list of student performance objectives and items testing mastery of those objectives from which they can choose the objectives of importance, without having to define them themselves. Such a pool is now being generated for grades 4, 5, and 6 mathematics, and it is expected that a similar pool of science objectives and items will also be generated in 1972 and 1973 at OISE. IOX, the Instructional Objectives Exchange (Popham, 1971), is already in existence and has gathered a varying number of objectives in at least fifteen subject areas, although companion test items are not available for all objectives.

A second alternative to actually specifying student performance objectives at initial stages of curriculum development is now being tried by a group of Project teachers working on a reading program. This group began by defining a hierarchy of reading skills necessary for comprehension. They are now searching for items that will test degrees of mastery of each of those skills at various grade levels. These items will form a diagnostic instrument that will indicate primary skills requiring emphasis and around which their new program can be built. Analysis of the choice of test items will indicate both the standards that teachers expect of their students and the conditions under which these standards are to be met. It seems likely that the diagnostic test will accelerate the initiation of the program and will facilitate the defining of objectives, since they can be deduced from an existing operational statement of their intent. This method has the further advantage of avoiding statements of unachievable objectives that at a later stage would retard the building of curriculum strategies.

The subjects mentioned thus far (reading, social studies, and mathematics) as programs based on clearly delineated objectives in the Project raise questions about the constraints that various content areas impose upon statements of student performance objectives. Although it is relatively simple to specify objectives in mathematics, languages, and science, in areas such as art or creative writing, where novel responses are desired, the particular behaviors to be developed cannot be specified until after instruction. In the sense that it becomes harder to define a nonarbitrary standard for assessing mastery and to attach content as well as behavior to objectives in such areas, this is a real problem. The issue has been clouded, however, by the nonequivalent comparisons typically made. There is both a skill and a creative aspect to both sets of subject areas mentioned. The criticism does not, in fact, apply to a subject as such, but rather to the creative or novel aspects of each subject. Furthermore, whether or not art or science is characterized as having a greater proportion of this creative quality depends entirely on how the subject is approached by the teacher. The question remains, then: are the creative components of a subject area amenable to behavioral specification? Ebel (1967) points out that to say that creative merit cannot be measured is equivalent to saying that "no verifiable statements regarding differences in quality can be made. If that were true what business would some people have in trying to educate other people in such matters? [p. 266]" This problem seems to be lessened, once again, when teachers are the ones involved in specifying the objectives. A group of teachers working on a creative writing program in the Project illustrate this point. They are concerned not so much with a general definition of creativity (which might be an impasse to a nonteacher group), as with identification of the criteria that they have previously employed intuitively in evaluating the differential writing quality of their students. Such an operational definition can be arrived at through objective analysis of writings previously judged to be of high quality.

The sixth stage in this process is evaluation of the curriculum as it develops. Evaluation may be both summative and formative, and multidimensional in nature. Given our present focus on program development and accountability, our main concern is with the problems raised with regard to formative evaluation of student achievement. One of the primary reasons for the recent interpretation of accountability as something new is its emphasis on student achievement in the cognitive domain (and, in some instances, the motor domain) rather than the affective domain, where the focus of many educators has tended to be in the past decade. The public wishes to know what the student can do after exposure to program X_1 that he could not do before, and how this change compares to the change that might have occurred had the student taken program X_2 instead.

The concept of student performance objectives was created specifically so that these questions could be answered. Yet doubts have been raised as to its ability to facilitate the necessary measurement. These doubts center on the differences between applying standards and making judgments, and the limitations of typical tests in assessing learner outcomes. Eisner (1967) questions the assumption that objectives can be used as standards for measuring achievement, since no clear distinction is made between the application of a standard and the making of a judgment. The former, he suggests, results in measurement, but the latter does not. Ebel (1967) points out, however, that all measurement involves comparison, but not necessarily the comparison of an instance (such as a behavior) with a standard. It may involve the comparison of two instances. The comparison of two instances requires the use of so-called relative criteria for the creation of the norm-referenced scores most common to present educational grading systems. Eisner's point is well taken, though, since a norm-referenced score results in the evaluation of individual students through ranking (percentile scores) but does not usually result in program evaluation. Program evaluation typically requires the use of absolute criteria that are the standards included in student performance objectives. When such criteria are used in criterion-referenced tests, the resulting scores indicate program objectives that are not being met and associated curriculum activities that are inadequate, thereby facilitating diagnosis and program revision. Eisner argues further that some modes of achievement cannot be measured in these terms. But teachers are constantly making judgments of these modes of achievement in grading, although usually in norm-referenced terms. Both norm-referenced and criterion-referenced measures are based on educational objectives, although these objectives are not often made explicit in cases where norm-referenced measures are used. The position put forward here is to make these criteria explicit, through the kind of operationalizing activities already discussed, so that their appropriateness can be judged by the user and communicated to the learner as well as other relevant persons in the educational environment. A criterion-referenced measure can be used for norm-referenced purposes also, and it enables the teacher to display results of achievement in highly visible terms. Objectives can be listed and checked off as they are achieved, providing a very thorough record of pupil progress, as evidenced in the Project and suggested elsewhere (Millman, 1971).

The instruments and items devised to evaluate mastery of objectives also have been subjected to criticism. Paper and pencil tests are often criticized, correctly, as being inadequate to the task. Performance tests also are not reliable records of behavior in a real problem situation, since the pupil knows the problem has been artificially contrived. While these shortcomings often exist, they are common to all educational testing situations and certainly cannot be considered an indictment of performance objectives for purposes of evaluation. Moreover, it may be possible under some conditions to observe mastery of objectives in more spontaneous circumstances, when the objectives are listed in such a way as to be checked off quickly.

Student performance objectives have been discussed at great length in the education literature and seem to have passed through alternate periods of acceptance and rejection by the profession. We have referred to many of the reasons for rejection as pseudo problems, and the periodic reacceptance of performance objectives provides evidence to support our criticism. The characteristics of the Project and the usefulness of performance objectives in this setting suggest that a major prerequisite for their operationalization is that they be chosen or generated by those directly responsible for implementation – the teachers. Given problem identification at this critical level, the logic of the use of student performance objectives is hard to deny. They are mechanisms that enable educators to indicate their intentions and to facilitate the measurement of the success with which these intentions are met. The recent call for accountability is essentially a request for the use of such a mechanism and the changes it may suggest.

THE DESIGN OF EDUCATIONAL EVALUATION

The differences between the purposes of educational evaluation and educational research make decisions regarding experimental design intriguing, to say the least. Stake and Denny (1969) have suggested that the major difference concerns the degree to which the findings are generalizable beyond their application to a given product or setting: "Almost always, the steps taken by the researcher to attain generalizability tend to make his inquiries artificial or irrelevant in the eyes of the practitioner. The evaluator sacrifices the opportunity to manipulate and control but gains relevance to the immediate situation [p. 374]." This is not to imply that manipulation and control are not often concerns of the evaluator; rather, the reason for manipulation and control in an evaluation study differs from that in a research study. Through appropriate experimental design, manipulation and control may provide a type of generalizability, but user-centered evaluation will also be required. Educational environments differ radically, and the number of unique variables found in the most "teacher-proof" curricula still far surpass the variables that can be held constant. The evaluator's concern for manipulation and control, then, is prompted by the desire, not to achieve generalizability, but to reduce the number of competing explanations that may be applied to data on a specific enterprise. In order to reconcile the need to deal with field conditions and requirements as they exist, at least some of the manipulation and control lost through the use of pre-experimental and quasi-experimental design will be replaced by the introduction of statistical control – analysis of covariance, for example – where the effects of uncontrolled variables on the dependent variable can be partialed out, in spite of the inequality of treatment and control groups on those dimensions.

In some cases, the introduction of any type of design other than a preexperimental one thwarts the purposes of the evaluation. Provus (1969) has suggested that experimental design is irrelevant to evaluation until a program is in its final stages. With most designs, beginning an evaluation of a program in its formative stages serves to deprive the development staff of their desired opportunity to improve the product on the basis of experience and may actually deny the staff the information required for product improvement.

This problem contributes substantially to the more general controversy over the utility of control groups in evaluation studies. Some of these controversies have been outlined by Cronbach (1963) and Forehand (1966), the most critical one being the lack of meaningful comparisons between new and traditional courses. Any evaluation of student achievement is either implicitly or explicitly based on the educational objectives of the treatment to which the student is exposed. Since the most meaningful comparisons of efficiency of different treatments in producing achievement on the same dimensions must be based on identical criteria, and since the criteria for such comparisons are educational objectives, achievement of the objectives of either the innovative or the traditional treatment must constitute the basis of these comparisons. Clearly such comparisons, in terms of gain scores, are in many cases invalid, since there is little reason to expect either similarity of goals or achievement of goals foreign to the intent of one of the two treatments or programs involved in the comparison. This lack of goal similarity presents fundamental problems to comparative educational evaluation. School programs often change, not so that they can better achieve their present objectives, but in response to larger social changes that dictate new instructional objectives. In such instances, the relevant comparisons to be made involve, at one level, student achievement in relation to program objectives and, at a more fundamental level, program objectives in relation to relevant social goals.

A closely related problem arises even before the above issue can be considered. Both treatments, but especially the traditional comparison treatment, may defy definition because of a lack of clearly stated goals, changing treatment characteristics, instructional flexibility that lowers the probability of accurate replication below an acceptable minimum, or a combination of these three factors. Even where such definition is possible, the assumption of comparability may result in an emphasis on traditional rather than innovative objectives. For example, an attempt to identify, for purposes of evaluation, the objectives of a traditional program may require a considerable expenditure of resources that is difficult to justify, particularly if the result of the expenditure should be the discarding of the product. Control groups may be extremely expensive in relation to their payoff. There is also the danger that many dimensions frequently subjected to comparative evaluation are matters of value judgment.

Because of these problems, evaluation strategies for the Project vary among noncomparative strategies, where new program objectives are installed; extensive use of internal comparisons; and a discriminating use of external comparison, where programs have been devised for the purpose of better achieving previously identified goals. As Scriven (1967) points out, it may be useful merely to know that treatments do differentially affect learner outcomes; although the causes of the difference may remain unidentified, this knowledge would warrant further scrutiny of causal factors and may, as a result, lead to a better understanding of program effectiveness.

The Choice of Design
One or more of three experimental designs have been used to assess student achievement in the Project. According to Campbell and Stanley's (1963) terminology, these may be described as (1) the one-group pretest–posttest preexperimental design, (2) the nonequivalent control group quasi-experimental design, and (3) an adaptation of the preexperimental static group comparison.

In 1970/71, the one-group pretest–posttest preexperimental design was used to evaluate student achievement in all the Project components. The information yielded by this design is limited by a number of extraneous variables that can jeopardize internal validity. In the Project, these variables include history, maturation, and the effects of testing. The effects of history and maturation are greatest in the case of the two packaged programs (IPI and Conceptual Skills), since there is a considerable lapse of time between pre- and posttesting. Results from the two locally built programs (mathematics and social studies) are influenced less by history and maturation than by the tendency of students to perform better on the second administration of the same or an alternate test. Since these extraneous variables often have an inflationary influence on true difference scores, there is a need for conservatism in the interpretation of results. But despite this shortcoming, the design is useful for evaluating both types of program. For the locally built curricula that are in the formative stages of development, it helps to promote program development – a major role for evaluation in this context. For the two highly developed packaged curricula, it permits teachers to develop the school-specific techniques required to make the program optimally successful. Further, the pressure of implementing a new curriculum in the first year could, under some circumstances, be added to by the knowledge of comparison. Teachers have enough difficulty determining how to operate a new program at a very basic level in the first year without having to be concerned with how its effect will compare with those of other programs.

The quasi-experimental nonequivalent control group design was used with pre- and posttesting in one instance in 1970/71. Socioeconomic status (as well as school size) was heavily relied on as a similarity criterion because of both its potency in relation to achievement variables (Ireton, Thwing, & Gravem, 1970) and the availability of such data without large resource expenditures. Depending to some extent upon the equivalence of groups on pretest scores, this design controls the main threats to internal validity of history, maturation, testing, and instrumentation, since these factors should influence control and experimental groups equally. Regression effects are not likely to occur since there is no need to be concerned with extreme groups.

The static group comparison design has been adapted to make it inexpensive, convenient, and practical to employ; it also yields unusually dependable comparative data for evaluation purposes. Typically, this design compares the posttest results of a group that has experienced a treatment with those of a group that has not, for the purpose of establishing the effect of the treatment. The major weakness of the design is that it offers no mechanism for determining initial group equivalence. The groups may differ even in the absence of treatment. In addition, as Campbell and Stanley (1963) point out, efforts to match groups on selected background characteristics are usually ineffective and misleading. The method of grouping subjects, then, is the major flaw in this design; but when it is overcome by randomization, this approach assumes the stature of a true experimental design.

Several evaluation studies in the Project have employed a compromise between these preexperimental and true experimental designs by assigning subjects to groups. The limitations of matching are well known, but they can be greatly reduced if a comparison group is chosen from an identical setting. Thus, comparison subjects for some programs are the pupils in the same grade, in the same school, and with the same teacher as in the prior year. For example, if an innovative kindergarten program introduced in September 1972 is to be evaluated with this design, the grade 1 children (the 1971/72 kindergarten class) will be posttested in September and these results compared with the results of the class taking the innovative program in June or September 1973. The assumption of pretest group equivalence cannot be accepted as readily in this instance as it could be if comparison and control subjects were randomly assigned. But given the relatively stable population from which the subjects are drawn, history is virtually the only confounding variable to a perfect group match. Some of the children will even have the same parents. Certainly, socioeconomic status (SES), IQ, motivation, teacher effects, school environment, and community environment will be common to both control and treatment groups. Accordingly, we would classify this design as quasi-experimental.

This design has a number of other advantages in its application to evaluation studies, the major one being its economy. Comparison groups are always difficult to find, and noninnovating schools are understandably reluctant to participate in studies for which they perceive few immediate benefits. Under the plan outlined above, both control and experimental groups can be drawn from the innovating school. If randomization techniques were employed instead, half of the target population would have to forgo the innovative treatment in order to serve as a comparison group; or alternatively, the treatment could be offered to only one-half of the target population for the first half of the year and to the remainder of the target population in the second half of the year. None of these requisites for randomization is convenient in the school context, and none is necessary with the design modification we have suggested.

Evaluating Student Achievement – Criterion-Referenced Measurement
Educational objectives stated in terms of student performance provide the tools for building achievement measures in this evaluation. Achievement measures differ from aptitude measures (such as IQ and motor educability). The latter are based on a demonstrated relationship between the present performance and the future func-

tioning of the individual in a specified domain of activity. Achievement measures are concerned with the properties of present performance compared with some continuum of knowledge (Glaser, 1963) that may be a curriculum. Such measures are therefore based either explicitly or implicitly on educational objectives (Jackson, 1970) and are structured in accordance with two general functions (Popham & Husek, 1969): providing a basis for making decisions about (1) individuals and (2) treatments or groups exposed to different treatments.

Measures designed for the purpose of facilitating selection decisions among individuals are labeled norm-referenced measures (Glaser, 1963; Popham & Husek, 1969; Cox, 1970; Lindvall & Nitko, 1969). Norm-referenced measures are based on hierarchical orderings of individuals using percentile ranks, age and grade equivalents, stanines, and standard scores in which the meaningfulness of the individual score depends upon a comparison with scores of other testees. Measures that are designed to determine an individual's mastery of an established criterion (objective) or the effectiveness of a treatment upon a group are usually labeled criterion-, content-, or domain-referenced measures. While in theory the content of these two types of measures appears to differ, in practice one measure may be effectively used for both functions (Cox, 1970), since most of the characteristic properties of norm-referenced measures that differentiate them from criterion-referenced measures are often incidental rather than necessary differences. Of the eight differences noted by Cartier (1968), for example, two are concerned with reporting and interpreting the derived score, three with testing procedures, and one with action taken on the basis of results. Only two of the reported eight differences would influence item selection in a differential manner, and both of these relate to test variability – the core issue in discussions of differences between the two types of achievement measures (Popham & Husek, 1969).

Because norm-referenced measures are designed for the purpose of discriminating among individuals, items are usually chosen that maximize variability. Items to which high achievers always respond correctly and low achievers respond incorrectly are considered most appropriate. One result of retaining items to which most students respond correctly is the addition of a constant to all scores; for this reason, such items are often eliminated. Cox (1965) has suggested, however, that statistical item selection alone is not sufficient, since the validity of any achievement test depends upon the correspondence between educational objectives and the extent to which they are measured – a correspondence that may be very small if statistical discrimination indices are the only tools used. A priori decisions need to be made about the number of items required to assess the achievement of each objective; then discrimination indices are applied only to the specified number of items derived from a larger pool generated for each objective. A likely result of such procedure is a reduction in variability of the norm-referenced measure, since it is highly probable that at least some objectives will be mastered by almost all students in spite of attempts to limit discrimination indices to intra-objective item selection.

While valid norm-referenced measures may have lower variability than is sometimes assumed, criterion-referenced measures may have potentially greater variability. Low variability is thought to be typical of criterion-referenced measures because the meaning of the score depends exclusively upon its relationship with an educational objective. Under hypothetical conditions where treatment groups achieve all program objectives, variability will be zero and traditional estimates of reliability, validity, and techniques of item selection based on standard deviation will be irrelevant (Cox & Vargas, 1966; Popham & Husek, 1969). The logic of this argument, however, is based on an assumption probably derived from large-scale curriculum projects and is not necessarily acceptable when teachers are involved, as they are in this Project, in specifying or selecting and evaluating objectives for their own programs. The assumption is that educational objectives themselves and the standards associated with each objective are constant for the total target population.

Packaged curricula often appear to operate on this assumption by allowing teachers to manipulate specified standards and objectives as their needs require, and by establishing minimal standards for the achievement of objectives (Glaser & Cox, 1968). Teachers building their own curricula, intimately familiar with the range of abilities of their target population, have less need to work within these constraints. In fact, they would be unnecessarily assuming perfect instruction, homogeneous grouping, or lack of individual differences if they did not specify hierarchical standards and vary their objectives in accordance with known ability differences in their students. Some students will never achieve some objectives, no matter what the standard, while others will derive much more from a curriculum than could reasonably be expected of the "average" student. For this reason, it is very likely that such measures will have considerable variability – perhaps as much as a test designed for norm-referenced purposes. In addition, there seems to be little merit in suggesting that traditional estimates of reliability be discarded on the basis of present theoretical information about criterion-referenced measure variability (Jackson, 1970). A more reasonable approach would be to make such a decision on the basis of the real variability to be found in a specific criterion-referenced measure. The issue seems to be more an empirical than a theoretical one at this point.

The issues of homogeneity and dimensionality help to highlight the fairly large shift in both technical and philosophic direction being taken by proponents of criterion-referenced measurement. Even to say that norm-referenced measures differ from criterion-referenced measures because the former use a relative and the latter an absolute standard is simplification to the point of inaccuracy, since a norm-referenced test based on a standardizing population is also an absolute measure in the sense referred to here. In an informative resource book for teachers of geography, Senathirajah and Weiss (1971) have begun to fill in a large gap in teachers' knowledge of evaluation procedures. The section of the book concerned with item analysis, however, promotes classic procedures that are inappropriate for the testing purposes of many practitioners. Although the authors point out that the procedures they describe are for purposes of discrimination and hence foster homogeneity of items, failure to discuss other purposes of evaluation and accompanying methodology leaves the teacher with no choice and thereby increases the likelihood that the item selection procedures will work against his interests in pupil diagnosis and program evaluation.

In fact, teachers are at least as interested in pupil diagnosis and program improvement as in pupil discrimination. But when traditional item analysis procedures are employed, these first two functions are thwarted. This is because these two functions require test items representative of the educational objectives of the curriculum, and hence a test that may be multidimensional. Classical item analysis procedures tend to make a test unidimensional or homogeneous by screening out the items that fail to correlate with the prevailing dimension. In the case of a standardized mathematics test, for example, the homogeneous nature of the test necessitates the assumption of some unitary mathematical dimension. The criterion-referenced measures used in this evaluation of IPI, however, assume many dimensions of mathematical ability and define those dimensions through the measuring instrument. The practice, then, of eliminating test items on the basis of discrimination indices that increase homogeneity (decrease dimensionality) has the effect of lowering test validity (Anastasi, 1961) by reducing criterion coverage when the purpose of the test is diagnosis or program evaluation.

Regardless of the choice of experimental design for the assessment of student achievement, the use of criterion-referenced measures represents a threat to external validity that merits comment here. External validity depends on the generalizability of experimental findings and may be jeopardized by at least four factors (Campbell & Stanley, 1963). One of these factors, the reactive or interaction effect of testing, is particularly important when criterion measures are used as pretests. In such instances, it seems reasonable to expect that student sensitivity and responsiveness to the treatment may be enhanced by testing that poses problems of central concern to the subsequent treatment. But when – as in IPI and the local mathematics programs – the criterion measures are employed diagnostically and, therefore, the tests are part of the treatment, the threat to external validity is removed.

Multiple-Matrix Sampling
A further issue related to the operationalizing of experimental evaluation design should be dealt with here. This concerns procedures for data collection – specifically the collection of criterion-referenced data. Collection of such data ideally includes a comprehensive assessment of student achievement of all program objectives, resulting in many test items. In most school settings, the amount of time required to test all students on all items becomes prohibitive. There appear to be two possible solutions to this problem, and both have been tried in the Project. One is to incorporate the testing into the ongoing program, using the items for teacher-diagnostic as well as overall evaluative purposes. This option has the advantage of providing immediate feedback to the teacher and is difficult to surpass as a formative evaluation strategy when the teacher is also the curriculum developer. Its disadvantages include inconsistent testing procedures, since there are many testers, as well as the placing of responsibility for carrying out the testing schedule largely on the shoulders of teachers. When the data are to be used for summative purposes, experience in the Project indicates that in spite of relatively open communication channels, the need to carry out the testing schedule and procedures exactly as planned may not be fully understood. This severely jeopardizes the reliability of the data.

A more satisfactory compromise seems to be the provision of diagnostic test items for use in the formative mode, as well as a formal testing program carried out by the evaluators themselves. In the latter case, techniques have to be found both to reduce testing time dramatically and to assess all program objectives. One apparently satisfactory method of doing this is to divide the total item pool into a number of subtests, each requiring about the same period of time to complete, and then randomly to assign them to students within a given class. This strategy results in a mean score for each item for each class rather than a score for each student. Such a result is particularly attuned to the purposes of criterion-referenced measurement, since the adequacy of the program in achieving each of its objectives necessarily becomes the focus of evaluation. Shoemaker (1972) has labeled this procedure multiple-matrix sampling.

Criterion-referenced measures frequently consist of large numbers of performance items that place heavy demands on the time of the evaluator if formal testing procedures are to be carried out. In this Project, the time of testers has been severely limited, resulting in a search for adequate methods of expanding the evaluation without reducing the quality of the data. In one program, a highly selected group of volunteer parents were trained in the administration of individual performance test items in science. From the evaluators' point of view, the data they collected were highly reliable as a result of the extensive training and monitoring of testing procedures. In fact, because parents were chosen who had children the same age as the subjects being tested, the rapport of tester and testee often surpassed the rapport that a professional tester would be able to establish. From the point of view of the principal implementing the program, the use of parents as testers had several added positive features. The parents, having become thoroughly familiar with the school operation in general and the new program in particular, acted as ambassadors of good will to the community for the school. Exposure to the school under structured conditions also added considerable impetus to the volunteer parent program.

THE PROJECT EVALUATION MODEL

Evaluation of the Project is a three-year endeavor for most existing components, expanding as diffusion occurs and as resources allow. The present purposes of the evaluation are threefold, the primary one being the determination of student achievement gains attributable to innovative curricula. Such assessment proceeds largely on the strategy of measuring the discrepancy between intended and attained student behaviors by generating criterion-referenced items from statements of student performance objectives, although results of some norm-referenced testing also are considered. The second purpose of this evaluation is to describe in some instances present attitudes, and in others changes in attitudes, of those directly involved in the programs. This purpose is based on the premise that although the curricular materials package is often the independent variable in educational evaluations, learner outcomes are highly dependent upon the attitudinally controlled behaviors of those persons interacting with the materials. Third, in response to issues raised by Cronbach (1963) and others, observational data are being gathered for the purpose of more objectively describing curricular treatments. These data are designed both to assist in diffusion by increasing program replicability and to identify the range of curricular features potentially responsible for both achievement and attitudinal changes.

The essence of the Project is the allocation to teachers of responsibility and authority for curriculum planning and implementation. The resulting climate for change has produced two distinct types of educational programs in the schools: the first is well-developed, imported curricula (such as IPI mathematics and the Bereiter–Regan Conceptual Skills Program); the second is curricula developed by small groups of teachers designed to fulfill the particular needs of their school (such as the mathematics and social studies programs).

The central distinguishing features between the two categories of programs in the Project dictate two roles that any evaluation of them must assume. The imported programs are characterized by a minimum number of substantive points about which teachers are free to make decisions; and for this reason, evaluation is predominantly summative in nature. It is designed to determine whether outcomes justify added expense and inconvenience associated with adoption. Teacher style, however, is a major source of treatment variability critical to learning outcomes, and some evaluation activities centering on this issue are essential. The data from such evaluation may be interpreted in either the summative or the formative modes. Because the locally designed curricula are in various stages of field testing, the formative role predominates in their assessment in an attempt to provide feedback on the basis of which revisions can be made. The diffusion model on which many of the future activities of the Project are based suggests, however, that some components of these curricula may be of immediate interest to other schools. These data may therefore be considered, as Scriven (1967) notes, to be summative assessments of the early forms of these still emerging curricula.

The evaluation model applied to these curricula is a three-dimensional one adopted from an evaluation of Computer Assisted Instruction completed by the Central Midwestern Regional Educational Laboratory Inc. (Evans et al., 1969). This model is illustrated in figure 4.

Evaluation of the Project was and is sufficiently different from that of Computer Assisted Instruction to warrant some changes in the basic model. These differences include concern with four curricula (and more in the future) rather than one curriculum; curricula that are sufficiently different in nature to warrant modification in each case; and more limited manpower.

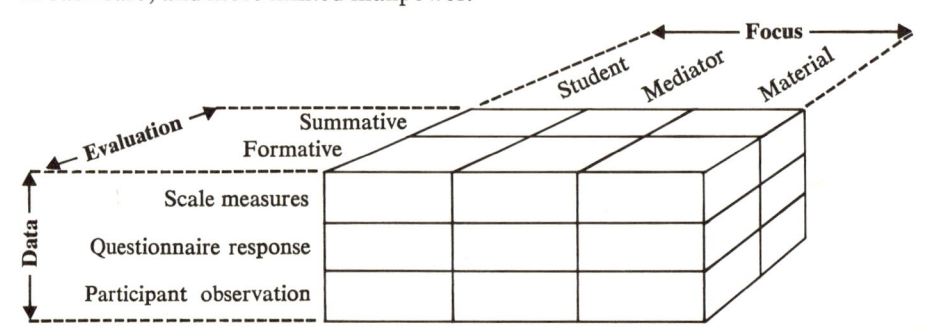

Figure 4. CEMREL evaluation model. *Source:* J. Evans et al., *Evaluation of computer assisted instruction* (St. Anne, Mo.: Central Midwestern Regional Educational Laboratory, 1969).

For example, the nature of the locally built curricula suggests that since a choice must be made, objective treatment observation data are more useful than participant observation data, particularly because of the smaller number of schools and close, relatively informal contact between the evaluator and the schools' principals and teachers. Lack of resources and the special characteristics of each curriculum dictate that many cells of the model for any given curriculum evaluation will be left empty. When the above modifications are made, the components of the evaluation of the Project, projected for a three-year period, are as shown in figure 5.

Data	IPI	Conceptual Skills	School C math	School A social studies
Achievement				
Criterion-referenced measures	1971 1972 1973	1971 1972 1973	1971 1972 1973	1971 1972 1973
Norm-referenced measures	1971 1972 1973		1971 1972 1973	
Observation of treatment	1971 1972 1973		1972 1973	1970 1972 1973
Attitudes				
Students	1971 1972 1973			1970 1972 1973
Teachers	1971 1972 1973	1971 1972 1973		
Parents	1971 1972 1973	1972		
Volunteer aides	1971 1972 1973		1971	1972
Baseline data	1971	1971		

Figure 5. Components of the evaluation of the Project.

CHAPTER 7

Evaluation of some project components

Four of the programs discussed in chapter 5 have been evaluated in varying degrees of completeness in relation to the Project evaluation model discussed in chapter 6. In the case of two locally built programs – School C mathematics and School A social studies – as well as the Conceptual Skills Program, evaluation focused exclusively on student achievement. In each case, criterion-referenced data were gathered and supplemented with socioeconomic status (SES) and IQ baseline data. Socioeconomic status was determined by father's occupation using Blishen's scale (1967). For all the kindergarten children in the Conceptual Skills Program, individual Stanford–Binet IQs were given by the TVC. For students in the other programs, Lorge–Thorndike IQs were available from school records. In the case of the math programs and the Conceptual Skills Program, standardized test scores were included (the Canadian Test of Basic Skills and the Slingerland Reading Test). The IPI math program evaluation included not only evaluation of student achievement, but also all the other evaluation components suggested by the TVC evaluation model.

The data and methodology presented here refer to the school year of 1970/71 and should be considered as first approximations to more extensive and complete data to be gathered for the subsequent two years. It should also be noted that a major portion of this chapter is devoted to an analysis of data on the IPI math program. This reflects the widespread interest in this program indicated by people outside the Project rather than the relative importance attached to it in comparison with other programs in the Project by Project personnel.

In 1970/71, the design employed in all programs but the Conceptual Skills Program was a preexperimental, pretest, posttest design. This design eliminated very few threats to the external validity of the evaluation results. When it was employed sequentially over a period of two or more years, however, the cumulative effect was the development of a time series design indicating that noted differences are due to the effects of the new programs.

The potential yield of information from this time series design is illustrated in figure 6. It is evident from this chart that the number of internal comparisons increases in proportion to the number of years in the programs. These comparisons can be made both horizontally and vertically, and are capable of partially answering two kinds of questions related to (1) the cumulative effect of the program on student mastery and (2) the influence of increased teacher efficiency on learner outcomes. All pairs of horizontal comparisons from grade 5 speak to the first issue (for example, B_1 versus A_2, C_1 versus B_2), although contaminated by the second issue. All pairs of horizontal comparisons at the grade 4 level (for example, A_1 versus D_1, A_1 versus E_1) speak best to the second issue and may provide an estimate of a constant increment that could be deducted from comparisons at later grades in order to increase the validity of the cumulative estimate of materials versus instructor influence. Since students in the schools using innovative programs up to grade 6 remain in the same schools through grades 7 and 8, comparison of achievement in a common program between students in innovative schools and those in traditional programs in other schools is not possible until the students reach grade 9. The earliest date at which this comparison can be made, therefore, is 1973/74; the full impact of the program cannot be determined, however, until 1975/76. It should be noted that comparisons of pretest data in grades 5 and 6 (A_2 versus B_1, B_2 versus

	Years			
Grade levels	1970/71	1971/72	1972/73	1973/74
Innovative program				
4	A_1	D_1	E_1	F
5	B_1	A_2	D_2	E_2
6	C_1	B_2	A_3	D_3
Regular program				
7		C_1	B_2	A_3
8			C_1	B_2
9				C_1

Figure 6. Information provided by a pretest–posttest experimental design when repeated over two or more years.

C_1) make it possible to estimate differences between the innovative and former programs in grades 4 and 5, since this situation is identical to the adaptation of the static group comparison design described in chapter 6.

SCHOOL C MATHEMATICS

Method

Administrative difficulties (such as time constraints and school schedules) with posttest data collection led to methods of data collection and analysis that were different from those originally planned, but nevertheless useful. The pretest criterion-referenced data were collected by administering all the test items for a given grade to all the students in that grade. This plan was carried through posttesting for the two grade 4 classes only. The grades 5 and 6 classes (two of each) were posttested by a multiple-matrix sampling procedure (see chapter 6), whereby the total number of test items was divided into ten subtests. Each subtest was then assigned, according to a table of random numbers to avoid selection bias, to two students in each class; and all tests were given simultaneously, using common instructions and test personnel at each grade level. The results indicate mean item achievement for each class but reveal nothing about the performance of individual students. Although the diagnostic function of the posttest is thereby lost, the technique has much to recommend it. First, it focuses evaluation on the program rather than the student. Second, it reduces testing time by 90 percent, since each pupil tries only one-tenth of the total number of items. And third, as a result of this, student motivation and response reliability are likely to increase.

In terms of the way the data are reported, this mixture of methods results in the following:

1. Pretest scores are all means derived from total student number (N) in each class.

2. Posttest scores are derived similarly for grade 4, but grades 5 and 6 mean scores are based on two students as selected through the randomization procedure.

3. Gain scores for grade 4 are calculated by subtracting pretest from posttest mean scores all based on the total class number. Grades 5 and 6 gain scores are calculated by subtracting pretest scores based on total class number from posttest scores based on a number of two as randomly selected.

4. Correlations, requiring individual responses for calculation, can be reported for only the grade 4 students.

Results

Much of the literature on criterion-referenced measurement suggests that test variability is likely to be very low or nonexistent; thus, classical methods of computing test reliability (that depend on test variability) are highly inappropriate.

It is nevertheless true that when a criterion-referenced test is devised by teachers for their specific objectives and students, (1) many objectives rather than a single objective are likely to be tested by the one test; and (2) test items are likely to reflect the range of objectives appropriate for the range of abilities available in most classes. This being the case, the appropriateness of classical procedures will depend upon empirically determinable test variability. School C's criterion-referenced tests were developed so that a split-half reliability could be determined, should variability exist. This was calculated for the posttests of the two grade 4 classes, which had standard deviations of 6.97 and 7.95. The split-half test reliability coefficient, with the correction suggested by Ferguson (1959, p. 282), was a very high 0.96 in each case.

Table 1 reports the criterion-referenced pretest, posttest, and gain scores for each class. The achievement of all program objectives would have resulted in a total possible score of 206 for grade 4, 191 for grade 5, and 156 for grade 6. The data indicate apparently substantial gains, although lack of comparative data makes this judgment a tentative one. The data also indicate a large variation between grade 5 classes in terms of the gains made. It is interesting to note that the class making the largest gains had the lowest pretest scores and the highest posttest scores, by a substantial amount. These results suggest significant differences in either teachers' effectiveness or teachers' objectives. They could also be accounted for by differences in time in which portions of the course were covered.

Tables 2, 3, and 4 indicate the specific skill areas accounting for both the greatest gains and the differences in gains between classes. Table 2 shows negligible difference between grade 4 classes in all skill areas and smallest gains in the areas of addition and subtraction. The latter finding can be explained by the time of test administration (late October), since addition and subtraction constitute the first parts of the grade 4 program. Largest gains are made in the areas of multiplication and division, and this is to be expected from the program emphasis.

Table 3 shows negative gain scores for one grade 5 class in the areas of addition, subtraction, multiplication, decimals, linear measurement, and volume measurement; and the positive gain scores from the other class are very low. In the case of the first four skill areas mentioned, ceiling effects resulting from the late pretest administration could easily account for the results. The existence of this feature necessitates more than the usual caution in data interpretation. One class, for example, has a very large negative gain score in the area of decimals (−8.43). Comparison of the pretest scores of the two classes suggests, however, that the class with the negative gain score had already covered the portion of the course in which decimals are included, whereas the other class had not. The negative gain score can probably be attributed to forgetting, and the two classes posttest at the same level (13.5). The only exceptionally large gain shown in the data is in the area of percent, all other gains being fairly modest when considered individually.

Table 4 indicates only two negative gain scores in the grade 6 classes, and these are of a very small magnitude.

Three features of the data in table 5 bear mention here. Both SES and IQ seem to have roughly the same relationship to the standardized test (CTBS) scores as the pretest and posttest criterion-referenced scores. SES accounts for 3 to 14 percent of the variance in both types of math scores, while IQ accounts for 26 to 49 percent of the variance. CTBS subscores are almost as strongly related to the criterion-referenced measures as they are to one another. The last column of table 5 shows the maximum correlation coefficient of 1.00 in several instances. These are due to the small number in those cells. This column also shows many negative correlations that are typical of correlations with gain scores and are rarely significant. The size of the correlations (−0.77, −0.54, −0.65) of the criterion-referenced pretest with the gain score, however, invites speculation. It suggests that children with high pretest scores have low gain scores. One factor influencing such a result, of course, is the tendency of the test to have too low a ceiling for high-achieving children and hence to give them little opportunity to demonstrate changes in their behavior resulting from program-stimulated learning on the posttest. Whether or not such a ceiling exists cannot be determined at this time. If it does not, one possibility is that the mathematics program stimulates students of average and low ability but does very little for those whose pretest indicates high achievement.

SCHOOL A SOCIAL STUDIES

The components of the program chosen by teachers for this evaluation were research skills. Fifty-nine objectives were identified by the teachers in that area and test items generated for each objective. Because the area being evaluated was a skill rather than content area, common objectives and items were used at the grades 4, 5, and 6 levels, although there was an exception of superior performance for each successive grade level.

Method

The evaluation plan called for both pretest and posttest administration of all test items by each teacher to his own class. This was done for the pretest, but on the posttest the following administrative problems were encountered:

1. One grade 6 teacher was unable to administer the posttest, and that class has been dropped from the present evaluation.

2. One grade 4 class changed teachers midway through the year, and results suggest that the objectives of the two teachers may have differed substantially.

3. The teacher of the above class and one grade 5 teacher omitted seven items from the posttest, so that these data are missing in those two instances.

Results

The last column of the last row of table 6 indicates that gain scores across all classes approached zero (0.62), a not unexpected result considering the time of testing. Because most of the fall term was spent in constructing objectives and later in generating test items, the pretesting did not take place until the end of January. It seems likely that much of the program's effectiveness for the year would have been measured by the pretest and that the posttest was, in most instances, a measure of retention. The teachers involved have suggested that the greatest instructional emphasis was placed on research skills during the time that they were determining their objectives in that area. Under such circumstances, the negative gain scores in three of the five classes may indicate only that some forgetting occurred.

The results for the two grade 4 classes are worthy of further discussion because of the differences between them in terms of IQ, pretest, posttest, and gain scores. Class 2 was the class that underwent a change of teacher, and research skills appear to have been neglected as a result. Class 1's performance, however, although slightly lower at pretest (21.46) than any of the grades 5 or 6 classes, surpasses them all at posttest with the largest gain recorded (5.73). This is the case even though the mean IQ for that class (94.33) is lower than any other class by at least 5 IQ points.

Correlation data indicate little of significance and hence are not reported.

CONCEPTUAL SKILLS PROGRAM

Method

The evaluation of achievement in the Conceptual Skills Program involved the non-comparative assessment of achievement using pretest and posttest criterion-referenced scores with the seven schools in the program in 1970/71 (three Core schools and four Study schools). It also included a comparative assessment of achievement between a subsample of two classrooms using the Conceptual Skills Program and two comparison classrooms. Both Conceptual Skills and comparison classes were equally balanced in terms of males and females, and the schools were chosen to represent both high and low socioeconomic areas in the city.

Because of teacher apprehension in the comparison schools, students were not selected on a random basis. Teachers preferred to choose students that they felt (1) represented a cross-section of ability in their classes, and (2) would respond in a testing situation. There are several well-known, serious dangers inherent in this method of selection. If the teachers even subconsciously chose to select superior students, they may have biased the results against their own programs, since a high pretest score makes it more difficult to obtain a high gain score. There is a distinct possibility of this being the case, since teachers preferred to select responsive students. Further, because choices were made early in the year, if the teachers attempted to select a true cross-section, they may have inaccurately diagnosed their students' abilities. In the first case, the experimental program would appear more effective than it actually was. In the second case, it is not possible to predict the outcome. In any event, considerable caution should be used in interpreting these data, although the comparison and experimental groups appear closely matched on IQ, SES, and criterion-referenced pretest scores. An analysis of variance has revealed no significant differences. A pretest–posttest nonequivalent control group design was employed. The primary achievement measure used was an individually administered Conceptual Skills criterion-referenced test.

Results
The general hypothesis investigated here is that there is a positive treatment effect on the students over and above the effect of the general school program. The criterion-referenced data from the comparative portion of this study are presented first, because they indicate the main consequences that are further elaborated by subsequent data and analyses. There were four schools in the subsample – two with the experimental treatment and two with the control treatment – and each pair contained one high SES and one low SES school.

Table 7 shows mean scores and standard deviations for all measures. These data are of interest because of the IQ standard deviations as well as the various test standard deviations. In the case of IQ, the high SES experimental group (High E) has a 19-point standard deviation level that is above average and tends to inflate correlations; the low SES experimental group (Low E) has a standard deviation much below average on IQ that tends to deflate all correlation coefficients as a result of the attenuated range. The standard deviation change in the High E score from pretreatment stage is from 16 points to 9 points, a substantial shrinkage. This could conceivably be attributed to a test or program ceiling, were it not for the fact that immediately below the High E group is the Low E group with a mean score of 164 and a standard deviation of 13.5. It is more likely true that the program as presented in the High E group has had a homogenizing effect on the students. Such an effect could be considered a disadvantage of the program, except that in the Low E school the reverse process has taken place and in the remaining schools there has been no effect on standard deviation. This particular array of data is important from the point of view of the claim that packaged materials produce frighteningly uniform results. These data suggest that, at least for the Conceptual Skills Program, there is no cause for concern on this point.

The primary conclusion of the Conceptual Skills evaluation results from the data in the second row of table 8. These data indicate that the mean differences between the experimental and the control group are large and statistically significant. Within the limitations imposed by the design employed and by the nature of the measurement device, the Conceptual Skills Program appears to have effected a gain in student performance beyond the level of gain that might be expected in the absence of the program.

Table 9 provides evidence of the conclusion from the third row in table 8, namely, that the advantage from the Conceptual Skills Program is neither stronger nor weaker for the high SES group than for the low SES group. Such a result is particularly significant in the light of some popular criticisms of the Conceptual Skills Program suggesting that its beneficial effects are confined to disadvantaged students.

It must be conceded at this point that the low SES groups possess an IQ mean that suggests they are rather select; but a careful study of individual cases (not shown) shows substantial gains for high and low IQ students as well as high and low SES students. Analysis of gain scores (not shown) confirms the conclusions drawn with respect to tables 8 and 9.

Table 10 indicates that the correlation coefficients between sex and other variables are uniformly small and seem to be balanced between positive and negative signs. Since there are only two units on the sex scale, 0 and 1, the zeroes for females and the ones for males, the most reasonable interpretation of the data is that there appear to be no relationships between sex and any of the other variables.

The correlations between pretreatment criterion-referenced scores and posttreatment scores within classes is interesting for the wide range of values displayed – a high of 0.80 and a low of 0.22. This difference may be explained in part by the high variance for the High E group and the low variance or attenuated range for the Low E group. In instances such as this, where the numbers are very small (20 and 15), it is possible for one or two unusual cases to weigh very heavily on the resulting coefficient. An analysis of the individual cases in connection with the Low E group indicates that 7 out of the 15 cross over the median point during the treatment period; hence, the low correlation coefficient is a true reflection of the variation in impact of the Conceptual Skills Program on the students in their particular group. Since the packaged material in the Conceptual Skills Program was identical from group to group, the wide variation in correlation coefficients is a reasonable indication that the variation in style from teacher to teacher produces a variation in impact of the program on the children concerned. Data such as these warrant a reassessment of the oft-claimed limitation of structured materials that they impose a straitjacket on the learning of individuals within the classes where these materials are applied.

The high negative correlations between pretest scores and change scores are likely the result of a ceiling on the test, on the program itself, or on both, and constitute evidence beyond that already accumulated in research literature of the need to use caution in the interpretation of change scores.

The relatively high correlations between pretest scores and IQ (0.32 to 0.53) indicate the modest relationship between the criterion and the Conceptual Skills Program, and general intelligence as measured by the IQ test. These correlations are in a safe range of correlations; safe because a higher level would indicate too much similarity between general intelligence and the criterion measure, while a lower coefficient would raise questions about the need to intervene on some variable that appeared to have no relationship at all with academic potential or IQ.

Table 11 shows the group means on main variables for all seven schools in the program. The most important data in column 1 are reflected in the pretest mean of 177 for School H. The implication here is that virtually all the students in School H had attained criterion performance before the treatment period began. It happens that this particular group consisted of grade 1 students; and on the basis of the high pretreatment scores, no treatment was provided. This particular instance of high pretreatment mean scores suggests that in some, if not in many, cases of grade 1 class groups, the students will be operating at criterion or near-criterion performance levels independently of the treatment program's being administered in kindergarten. Critics of the Conceptual Skills Program may correctly view such data as an indication that through the elapse of time and the administration of the typical kindergarten programs, children will normally acquire the criterion performance skills. The main body of data in this report indicates, however, that many students begin the kindergarten year at a low level of performance on the criterion measure, and they can be brought to criterion performance levels more effectively if the Conceptual Skills Program is used than if it is not. Time and careful study will provide an answer to such basic questions as how long the advantage of the Conceptual Skills Program persists in those who benefit from it, and what the nature of the effects of these benefits is on such variables as reading.

The third set of figures here shows the uniformly high level of gains achieved by the schools receiving the Conceptual Skills treatment; virtually all of them are more than double the gains achieved by the control schools cited in earlier tables.

Correlation coefficients (not shown) computed for all schools in the program largely support the data reported in table 10. Perhaps the most important correlation coefficients for all schools are those between pretest criterion and the Slingerland reading subtests. These coefficients range from 0.04 to 0.30, with four of them being above 0.23. The correlations corresponding to posttest scores are slightly higher, and both sets are important because they indicate the degree of relationship between the criterion measure and reading. In order to assess the degree of relationship between the criterion test and the reading tests, it is necessary to look at the magnitude of the correlations among the subtests of the reading test. They range from 0.16 to 0.57, a somewhat higher range than the coefficients between the criterion measure and each of the subtests. The criterion measure, then, has a modest degree of relationship to reading as defined by the Slingerland tests. As in the case of the relationship to IQ, the correlations are in the safe range. If they were much higher, one could claim that the criterion measure is nothing more than a reading test; and if they were much lower, one could suggest that there is so little relationship to reading that the criterion measure may deal with a factor that is unimportant. It is clear that the criterion measure is reasonably associated with general intelligence and with reading, however it is not so strongly related to either that it could be identified as one or the other.

In summary, the Conceptual Skills treatment has had a significant impact on the students who participated in the program. The magnitude of this impact as measured by the criterion test is at least twice as great as the impact of kindergarten programs comparable to those in the control schools. The criterion test measures a variable that is related to but not identical to IQ, and related to but not identical to reading. The impact of the program is not uniform across all students, and there is strong evidence to indicate that the lack of uniformity is unrelated to either socioeconomic status or IQ. The Conceptual Skills Program can therefore be presumed to be effective for all students who show pretreatment performance levels that are below the criterion performance level.

INDIVIDUALLY PRESCRIBED INSTRUCTION: MATHEMATICS

Evaluation of IPI mathematics in the Project included all of the components of the Project evaluation model described in chapter 6. Among these are assessments of (1) student achievement, including both standardized and criterion-referenced measures; (2) observations of classroom activity, in this case pupil activity; and (3) attitudinal data from all those directly involved in the program (students, teachers, teacher aides, and parents). In the last case, several different methods of data collection were used, reflecting appropriateness for the information being gathered as well as the specific wishes of the school staff who will use the data in a formative manner.

Method
Student achievement. The effects of the IPI mathematics program on student achievement were assessed using, as a measure of the dependent variable, both standardized and criterion-referenced tests. Bialek and Castro (1968), Fisher (1967), and Research for Better Schools (1968), using the Iowa Test of Basic Skills, have found either no significant differences in mathematics achievement between IPI and control classes, or differences favoring the control schools. Oliva, Maguire, and Pacey (1971), using the Canadian Test of Basic Skills (a Canadian revision of the Iowa test), also have noted significant differences favoring control groups. Similar results have been obtained by Fisher (1967), using the Metropolitan Achievement Test, and Gallagher (1968), using the Stanford Achievement Test. The problems involved in using standardized, homogeneous measures to evaluate curricula have been discussed, in theoretical terms, in chapter 6. The issue revolves around the high probability that standardized instruments include test items measuring objectives that are not part of the curricula being evaluated or do not include items measuring many of the objectives that are in the curricula. Where such measures are employed, the results provide some indication of how well these curricula achieve the objectives of the standardized test but do not indicate how well the curricula achieve their own objectives. For many purposes, such standardized data are useful; for purposes of curriculum evaluation, their value is minimal. This is notably the case for innovative curricula containing novel objectives whose probability of assessment by a standardized test is particularly low. The evaluation of the success of a curriculum in achieving its objectives, then, is validly undertaken only by using criterion-referenced measures. In the case of IPI mathematics where this has been done using the "Placement Test" (Bialek & Castro, 1968; Research for Better Schools, 1968), students in the IPI program have scored significantly higher than control students.

Although the present data do not include a basis for comparison in criterion-referenced terms, noncomparative IPI student achievement is reported in this way. Other components in this section of IPI evaluation include correlations of IPI achievement with CTBS scores, IQ, and socioeconomic status; and year-end placement of IPI students by level for each grade and a comparison of year-end placements with those found by Oliva et al. (1971) and Scanlon, Weinberger, and Weiler (1970).

Table 12 indicates that the eight measures associated with student achievement in this study were socioeconomic status, IQ, pretest, posttest, and gain measures on IPI mathematics, and CTBS Arithmetic Concepts, CTBS Problem-solving, and CTBS total score.

All measures of IPI student achievement reported in this study are in terms of either numbers of specific IPI mathematics objectives achieved by students or levels within the program achieved by students. The pretest score was derived by transferring the placement level of each student as indicated by the placement test into the number of objectives represented. Similarly, the posttest score is the level reported on the student's record profile at the end of the program transposed into objectives. The gain score is the difference between the number of objectives achieved at pre- and posttestings. Means and standard deviations are reported for each of these measures. In terms of student achievement, the main questions center around the size of the gain made by students and differences in that gain (1) among grades, (2) among classes, (3) between sexes, and (4) among schools. The size of the gains made by IPI students (mean, 48.32) is difficult to interpret without direct comparative data, so that further clarification will have to await reporting of the 1971/72 evaluation.

There seems to be some systematic difference in mathematics achievement levels among grades. CTBS mean scores as well as IPI pretest, posttest, and gain mean scores show almost no differences between grades 4 and 5. One interpretation of these results is that the grade 4 math program in schools B and E in the previous year, prior to IPI, may not have been effective in teaching very much mathematics beyond what had already been learned, at least as far as any of these measures could determine. In fact, the strong suspicion that this was so was a major factor in the teachers' decision to adopt IPI mathematics. Another interpretation of these data is that the measures used did not accurately reflect the objectives of the earlier program. It is also interesting to note that given approximately the same starting point in IPI math, grade 4 students learned roughly the same material as rapidly as or slightly more rapidly than grade 5 students, posttesting at about the same level. While differences between grades 4 and 5 were very small on all mathematics measures shown in table 12, differences between grades 5 and 6 were substantially larger. This would appear to indicate a more effective grade 5 program in the previous year in terms of measured objectives and a slightly faster learning rate (grade 6 mean gain = 52.72 as compared with grade 5 mean = 45.13 and grade 4 mean = 47.99). The differences in gain scores are not large, however, and may be a function of program component difficulty differentials, testing effects, or chance variations.

At each grade level, pretest IPI scores favor males, a gap that appears to widen with age and is particularly large at the grade 6 level (twelve objectives) considering a difference in IQ of 6 points favoring females. While this difference still exists at the grade 6 posttest level (males, 139.80; females, 125.17), it is important to note that the gain scores are very close (males, 54.12; females, 51.33), suggesting that the relative cumulative deficit often apparent with female students in mathematics appears to have been retarded in the IPI program at the grade 6 level.

Differences between schools B and E on IPI gain scores are approximately the same in grades 4 and 5, and slightly favor School E at the grade 6 level. This may be accounted for by a regression effect, since pretest grade 6 IPI scores substantially favor School B (as do the CTBS scores to a lesser extent). Alternatively, the level of difficulty of objectives achieved by School B may have been higher since they were at a higher level in the program. Nevertheless, because pretest IPI scores favor School B at grade 5 also, it seems reasonable to suggest that the objectives of School B before implementing IPI may have been closer to IPI objectives than were those of School E.

Table 12 indicates few important differences among classes. The difference between the two grade 6 classes at School E, however, supports the contention that although the IPI program is highly structured, teacher functioning may create achievement differences. The difference in gain scores (61.83, 53.77) is approximately 8, favoring the class with the lowest mean IQ (93.87 versus 97.63), which also scored highest on the posttest (125.17 versus 119.35), even though it was slightly behind on the pretest (63.69 versus 65.65).

Column 10 of table 13 shows the correlations of IPI gain scores with the other variables included in the study. The variable with which there seems to be the smallest relationship is socioeconomic status. A much stronger relationship exists between IPI gain scores and IQ, being of the order of 0.61 for males and 0.53 for females at the grade 4 level (data not shown). Over all grades for the three IPI measures (the last three columns), IQ accounts for 10 to 40 percent of the variance; while in the case of the CTBS scores, IQ accounts for 20 to 60 percent of the variance, correlations being as high as 0.78 at the grade 4 level (data not shown). There is a systematic reduction in the relationship of IQ to both CTBS and IPI achievement from grades 4 to 6. This low relationship, at grade 6 at least, can be partially explained by teacher effect, as mentioned earlier. One grade 6 teacher (table 12) in particular discounted IQ as a related factor (by appearance) because of his class's high gain scores, high CTBS scores, but low IQ scores.

At the grade 4 level, IPI gain scores appear to have a reasonably strong relationship with all CTBS measures, and the reduction in this relationship to almost zero at the grade 6 level may again be partially accounted for by teacher effect. The extremely strong relationship between IPI posttest and gain scores is to be expected (Campbell & Stanley, 1963) and is accounted for by greater testee interest in the posttest as a result of participation in the program.

Table 14 records student placements, by level, for each school in both grades combined. The purposes of these data are to provide a comparison for the same schools in the subsequent year, when they will have become more experienced in the operation of the program, and a comparison with schools both in the Alberta study reported by Oliva et al. (see table 15) and in Oakleaf School, where IPI was developed (see table 16). Students in the Alberta study at the grade 4 level placed almost exclusively at levels D and E, while students in this study most frequently placed at levels C and D, with a substantial number – especially in School B (not shown) – at level B. Such data are difficult to interpret when neither pretest levels nor mean IQs are reported in the Alberta study. One may conjecture, however, that the relatively low mean IQs of the children in this study were lower than the IQs of the children in the Alberta study. This, coupled with the fairly strong relationship between IQ and IPI achievement, suggests lower pretest as well as posttest levels for children in this study. Only at the grade 4 level, however, are lower gain scores strongly suggested. Children in this study generally placed a level behind those in the Alberta study at the grade 5 and 6 levels also. When the data in table 14 are compared with data from both the Alberta study and the Oakleaf study (tables 15 and 16), substantial differences may be seen. These differences generally support the earlier contention that children in this study are approximately one level behind the Alberta or Oakleaf students.

These student achievement data seem to suggest reasonable progress with the IPI program. The increase in comparative data generated by the design described earlier should prove useful in the 1971/72 evaluation, but present data indicate that continued support for the program is warranted until the later findings become available.

Student attitudes. The success of the IPI mathematics program in Project schools will depend to a considerable extent upon the attitudes of the students toward the program. What these attitudes are likely to be is not easily determined, since there is at present some disagreement about the effect of the structure of the program. On the one hand, it has been suggested that the program is mechanistic, severely restricting the range of pupil activities in relation to mathematics. On the other hand, proponents of the program point to the freedom available to the student to proceed at his own rate and to vary the mathematical challenge according to his own abilities. Previous studies conducted by the program developers, Research for Better Schools, Inc. (1969), have indicated that (1) as reported from interview data, IPI pupils liked school better than non-IPI pupils; (2) IPI pupils liked math better than non-IPI pupils; and (3) in one instance, the implementation of IPI math in a ghetto school was accompanied by a significant reduction in vandalism and juvenile crime in the school. This generally positive attitude toward the program has been found elsewhere by independent evaluators (Oliva et al., 1971), who also suggest that it is very unlikely that students are able to separate their attitudes toward IPI math from their attitudes toward their school program generally.

The student attitude component of the 1970/71 IPI evaluation was undertaken to determine student opinion of IPI both as a separate component and in relation to other program components. In a sense, the issue of student nondiscrimination among components was being tested, but with the suspicion that in School E (School B will be included in the 1971/72 evaluation) the recency and method of implementation and the number of other innovations contributed substantially to individual component visibility. The staff at School E were also, of course, very much interested in student opinion of their innovations in addition to IPI mathematics.

Opinions were collected from pupils in the seven grades 4, 5, and 6 classes (total number, 205) at School E, using a liberally modified version of a questionnaire developed for a previous Project study (Montgomery, 1970). Modifications in the questionnaire were made to accommodate different innovations and staff interests; but the basic format, including the use of a Likert-type 5-point scale, a lie scale, and the style of wording questions, remained the same. The lie scale consisted of a series of control questions. Each time a student was asked for his opinion of an innovation, he was also asked for his opinion of the opinion of someone else (parent, peer, and so on) about the same innovation. The relative discrepancy of the two responses gives the researcher an index of the probable truthfulness of the student's reply.

The questionnaire consisted of fifty-six questions, each of which fell into one of three categories:

1. Student opinion of program innovations (including four questions concerning IPI mathematics).

2. Student opinion of innovative student grouping techniques. In this category, from responses to questions relating to "working alone" and "increased individual freedom," we may infer student opinion of some of the structural features of IPI math.

3. Student opinion of community involvement.

Results from the questionnaire as a whole indicate that of the fifty-six ratings made on the 1 to 5 scale, only thirteen fell below 4.0, the lowest being 3.5, still considered a moderately favorable rating. The mean rating for all questions was 4.2, with a rating of 4.4 and 4.2 respectively for the two questions (numbers 39 and 40) addressing feelings about school in general. Pupil and control question responses differed by 0.4 in two instances, 0.3 in two instances, and 0.2 or less in all other cases. Mean differences on items among classes were typically not large. In terms of ratings for individual innovative components, students gave IPI mathematics the highest mean rating (4.9), slightly ahead of field trips (4.8) and guest speakers (4.7). The lowest mean ratings were given to cross-grade grouping (3.4) and the discovery period (3.5).

The results of the opinion survey seem to indicate a very favorable attitude toward school generally and the IPI program in particular, and are in accord with earlier findings (Research for Better Schools, 1969; Oliva et al., 1971). The close correspondence between pupil and control questions also suggests that the responses are reasonably reliable.

The slightly lower grand mean ratings for items to do with student groupings, as compared with innovative programs or community involvement, may be related to the issue of visibility raised by Oliva et al. (1971). Both innovative programs and community involvement seem to be more easily identified as unique by students than are variations in classroom groupings. Should this be true, these high ratings can be attributed in part to high profile, in which case – although they are reliable – the responses may lack desirable validity (ratings may be of visibility rather than desirability). This could, in fact, explain a portion of the high ratings given IPI mathematics, the most visible, unique, and new component to be rated by the students, and the low ratings given the discovery period. Informal observation verifies the popularity of IPI math at School E, but the issue of visibility combined with natural student enthusiasm for a new activity suggests a need for conservatism in interpreting results in the first year of the program's operation.

Classroom observation of pupil activities. The purposes for which the observations of pupil classroom activity were undertaken correspond in part to the rationale outlined by Yeager and Lindvall (1968), who also devised the observation schedule used in this study. Where evaluation functions in a formative role, a variety of other data are essential to the interpretation placed on achievement data and provide a basis for future modification of program management, if not materials modification. These other data may concern program plan, teacher performance, and student activity. Although data on the last typically are missing from a majority of evaluation research, their value to the improvement of ongoing programs and further diffusion is considerable. IPI mathematics relies almost exclusively on individual student activity, a large portion of which is independent work differing radically from traditional classroom activity. Significant amounts of time spent on non-instructional activity may have serious negative effects on student outcomes, the reasons for which would not be objectively detectable in many ways other than systematic pupil observation.

Program replication in other classrooms and schools is heavily dependent upon such a description of treatment, also. Although IPI mathematics is not likely to be adopted in more schools in the near future, primarily because of current costs and reduced educational expenditures, staff turnovers in present user schools make a mechanism for replication necessary. Instructions to teachers, provision of materials, and assessment of achievement do not ensure that the program in two classes will be the same, even though these components may be common. Hence, while most programs will require modification for local conditions, lack of observation data precludes much systematic manipulation of treatment to meet these conditions. In short, observation data are being collected in this evaluation to develop a profile of student activity to be used in (1) interpreting achievement data and providing a basis for decision making about program revision, and (2) assisting in the replication of the program in other classes by other teachers.

The subjects of the observation were the thirteen classes of students in the IPI mathematics program at School B (180 students) and School E (205 students). Observations took place in regularly scheduled mathematics periods with no disruption of routine except for the presence of the two outside observers, who remained as unobtrusive as possible, spending the majority of their time at the perimeter of the classrooms. Each classroom was observed on three separate occasions by the two observers concurrently (interrater reliability, 0.79). The scores from the three observations for the two observers were used to compute a mean score that served to describe the pupil activity for a given class. Observers were trained in the use of the instrument by the investigator and given three practice sessions (these sessions also helped to reduce the reactive influences of their presence), after which problems of administration were discussed in detail and an attempt made to ensure that the same student behaviors would be recorded identically by the observers. The instrument developed by Yeager and Lindvall (1968) was used without modification.

Table 18 clearly indicates that over 96 percent of the observed pupil time was spent on either independent work or noninstructional activity. This corresponds with 90 percent and 82 percent reported by Yeager and Lindvall on a field laboratory school and an example adopting school respectively (see table 17).

In comparison with the data reported for the field laboratory school, the Project schools spent approximately 5 percent less time in independent work and 10 percent more time in noninstructional activity. While this comparison suggests areas for improvement, the discrepancy is far from irreducible. Further, when the Project schools are compared with the example adopting school, it appears that the Project schools spent about the same percentage of time on noninstructional activity and somewhat less time on teacher-pupil activity (11.84 percent for the adopting school as compared with 4.00 percent for Project schools), but about 14 percent more time doing independent work.

In spite of the reasonably favorable observation results of the Project IPI programs in relation to reported data from other IPI math programs, the 40 percent of time devoted to noninstructional activity is a highly visible and disconcerting component of the program to the Project teachers involved. Much of the cause appears to be the piling up of unmarked tests and unwritten prescriptions toward the end of each math program as a result of insufficient manpower. An attempt was made in 1970/71 to increase the marking manpower by increasing the number of volunteer aides to each school. It soon became evident, however, that increasing marking speed would not alleviate the piling up problem unless the prescription writing rate increased accordingly. Since prescription writing is the teacher's responsibility, this alternative was discarded as unworkable. Another solution proposed by the teachers was a reduction in the length of the IPI period by ten minutes (the time during which much of the noninstructional activity occurs), with that time being spent in mathematics drill – an activity that some teachers feel is neglected by the IPI program.

Teacher attitudes. While acceptance of an innovation by all those affected is essential to successful implementation, the commitment of the teacher to the worth of the innovation is probably most critical. In large part, it is the teacher's skill in program management and pupil motivation that determines achievement of some educational goals but not others, given equally sound program alternatives. IPI mathematics is reasonably unique from the point of view of the teacher's role, not just because it is individualized, but because of the manner in which the individualization occurs. Some observers, viewing the teacher's roles in IPI, have suggested that they are not consistent with normative conceptions of teaching in that they do not require the skills of the teacher. Clearly, the teacher does not adhere to traditional teacher modes of functioning in IPI. Nevertheless, the teacher's roles do require considerable skill of a type that must be classified as highly professional.

Lindvall and Bolvin (1970) have suggested that the teacher in IPI performs three major functions: operating the system, supplementing the system, and enriching the system. While operating the system is only one part of the teacher's role, it is of course extremely important. It consists of seven facets:

1. Evaluating and diagnosing pupil needs and progress.

2. Developing individual student study plans or prescriptions.

3. Developing immediate and long-range study plans for the whole class, allowing for individual differences.

4. Managing the classroom to make it an effective learning environment.

5. Planning large-group instruction in cooperation with other staff members.

6. Supervising the work of teacher aides.

7. Studying and evaluating the total system for the purpose of continuously improving its overall operation. One of the key ways of improving system functioning is through the training of pupils in the management of their own activities.

The teacher supplements the system by adjusting learner programs to meet learner characteristics identifiable only through daily student–teacher interaction. It is occasionally important for the teacher to "take exception" to the system by modifying its operation (for example, by lowering mastery requirements on a skill) to account for pupil characteristics that would otherwise detract from goal achievement. The teacher also has the opportunity to enrich the system by acting as counselor and as a selective reinforcing agent, thereby potentially contributing to the achievement of personal–social goals on the part of the student. In summary, the number of functions the teacher may perform in IPI is large, the skill required to perform them is considerable, and their nature clearly can be classified as professional.

The purpose of this examination of teacher attitudes was, first, to determine overall opinion of the program from those persons closest to all aspects of it after five and ten months' use; second, to pinpoint problems with the program from the teacher's point of view; and third, to weigh the relative advantages and disadvantages of the program as seen by the teachers. Implicit in these three purposes is the assumption that generally positive attitudes toward the program also indicate satisfaction with teacher roles. Negative attitudes may be confined to specific program components but may also include dissatisfaction with teacher roles. Where problems are noted but general opinion remains positive, however, satisfaction with teacher roles can be inferred.

Questionnaires adapted from an evaluation of teacher opinion of Computer Assisted Instruction (Rigsby & McIntyre, 1969) were administered to IPI teachers in School B (six teachers) and School E (seven teachers) in January 1971 and again in May 1971. Although a questionnaire in September 1970 would have been useful as an index of preprogram implementation opinion, the evaluation was undertaken too late to make this possible. As a means of ensuring a high response frequency, the questionnaire forms were distributed to the teachers by their principal, who strongly urged that they fill them out and gave assurance that their responses would remain anonymous. No name appeared on the forms, which were accompanied by stamped, self-addressed envelopes to the Trent Valley Centre, and no attempt was made to identify respondents other than by school.

It is important to note that in spite of the above procedures designed to ensure high response frequency, only three out of six teachers from School B returned the forms from the January or the May administration. Five of the six teachers from School E responded each time.

The teachers' general opinion of IPI mathematics both in January and May was that in spite of some problems, which they could readily identify, the program was effective and there was unanimous agreement on the use of the program for another year. This desire to continue was reinforced by the feeling that the program worked better later in the year than it did in the early part of the year, and probably suggests an investment of effort and acquisition of program management techniques whose benefits the teachers would be reluctant to lose. Even parents were generally perceived to be more interested in the school as a result of IPI. Teachers were somewhat reluctant, however, to express an opinion about extending IPI methodology to other subjects without further information about the specific programs and costs of implementation. Their generally favorable opinion of the program is consistent with the opinion of teachers using the program in other settings (Cox et al., 1966; Oliva et al., 1971).

The most frequent problems encountered by teachers using the program were late arrival of materials from the program developer and efficient utilization of "down time." Neither problem, however, was considered a threat to student achievement or motivation. As noted in the section reporting observation of pupil activities, this noninstructional use of time accounted for nearly 48 percent of pupil activity during the period devoted to IPI mathematics. The main reasons for this were identified by the teachers as lack of time for them to write prescriptions and the need for more markers, which, if remedied, would greatly improve the program. In spite of these problems, teachers at both School B and School E suggested a large number of common advantages to both teachers and students as a result of working with IPI. Teachers benefited by becoming more aware of a logical sequence in mathematics, being better able to diagnose individual needs, and having a lighter marking load, expertly prepared curriculum materials, and less work in preparing lessons. In the teachers' opinion, students benefited by being made aware of their own strengths and weaknesses, and by experiencing increased enjoyment and more independence and responsibility for program materials.

In the opinion of the teachers who answered the questionnaire, IPI mathematics is a reasonable success, justifying its costs and offsetting its attendant problems. The 50 percent response from teachers at School B, however, makes it difficult to interpret overall teacher opinion at that school. At best, failure to respond suggests lack of understanding of the purposes of program evaluation. At worst, it may indicate minimum interest or a negative attitude toward the program that the non-respondents are not anxious to make public. The responses received, nevertheless, imply complete familiarity with all aspects of the teacher roles mentioned by Lindvall and Bolvin (1970), coupled with satisfaction that those roles are of a professionally satisfying nature. This supports earlier data on teacher attitudes (Research for Better Schools, 1967), which characterized the teacher's role in IPI as more important than in traditional settings and viewed IPI as a step toward a superior classroom with specific strengths including materials, motivation of pupils, and the roles of the teacher.

Parent volunteers' attitudes. The first purpose of this aspect of the study was to determine the parent volunteers' opinions of the worth of the IPI mathematics program. Parent volunteers have a potentially unique perspective on the program, being exposed to it both as parents whose children constitute the program's clients and as para-professionals (in some respects) with at least some knowledge about the program, if not a vested interest in it. This dual role gives them the opportunity of making comparisons of program worth unavailable to other groups associated with the program.

The evaluation was also designed to determine parent volunteers' opinions about their own role in the IPI program. Because parent volunteers are heavily depended upon as manpower support for the program, their continued involvement is essential. These data are used in the formative mode to ensure job satisfaction and to avoid role assignments that would jeopardize the parent-volunteer program. To date, parent volunteers have been used almost exclusively as test markers, situated in either the IPI materials room (School B) or the corridor (School E). They also have assisted pupils in finding materials. Their rapport with teachers is generally reported to be very good, and they have access to the staff rooms of both schools.

The determination of pupil opinion about the IPI math program as perceived by the parent volunteers was a part of this evaluation component as well. The volunteers overhear many comments from students in the program that may be more candid than those the teachers hear, because the parent volunteers lack the aura of authority surrounding the teacher. These comments may bear more directly on the program than comments to parents at home, since the students are participating in the program at the time the comments are made.

A questionnaire, derived from an evaluation of Computer Assisted Instruction (Rigsby & McIntyre, 1969), was distributed by the principals to 14 parent volunteers at School B and 7 volunteers at School E. The questionnaires were accompanied by a stamped, self-addressed envelope to the Trent Valley Centre, and assurance was given that the respondent would remain unidentified. Questionnaires were returned by 8 of the parent volunteers at School B and by 5 of the parent volunteers at School E. In all cases, the questionnaires were completed correctly.

As was the case with the results of the teacher opinion survey, the number of parent volunteer respondents from School B was low, and similar cautions in data interpretation are recommended. Volunteers from the two schools were in accord in their opinion of the worth of the program, however, almost unanimously endorsing its superior effectiveness in contributing to student achievement as compared with previous programs in which their children had been involved. Probably their greater knowledge of and investment in the IPI program contributed significantly to this opinion. Reasons given for its effectiveness centered on aspects of individualization primarily as they contributed to positive student affect and did not include the expertly prepared program materials.

The parent volunteers expressed considerable satisfaction with their own roles, rating the work as definitely interesting and being quite prepared to volunteer again. The responses of several volunteers to the "necessary" rather than "rewarding" features of the routine of marking suggest that the stimulation of the children and the school environment generally may have played a major role in their perception of their fairly tedious marking jobs as being satisfying.

There appears to have been a total absence of the teacher–volunteer conflict reported in several instances in Alberta by Oliva et al. (1971). This may partly be due to a minimum of interaction because of geographical distance in the schools and partly to early expectations given the volunteers by the principals. In fact, the extremely favorable responses elicited by this questionnaire may, in some respects, be attributable to the volunteers' interpretation of their responsibility to the school and the professionally ethical behavior they were asked to assume upon taking part in the program.

Two significant features are evident in the volunteers' opinions about student impressions of IPI. The first is the enthusiasm and enjoyment the students experience while participating in the Project, and the second is the competitive attitude toward achievement that the program seems to have fostered. Individualizing the rate of progress only may serve to purify considerably the competitive environment of the "traditional" mathematics program. In effect, all students are placed on a standardized track with a visible beginning and end, and are allowed to run as fast as they wish. A more typical mathematics program not only does not have a standard track, but may have as many tracks as there are students. Furthermore, the speed of some participants over their own track is artificially regulated. All this serves to contaminate the competitive environment. While many educators will judge the highly competitive aspects of this program as undesirable, there is nevertheless (or as a result) substantial student enthusiasm for the program. Perhaps the student's option of competing only with himself enables those who do not often win when competing with others to experience an internalized feeling of success that is motivating.

Parental opinions of IPI mathematics. The dependence of schools upon public support is a prime motivation for this component of the IPI evaluation. School change that does not have, or fails to elicit, the support of parents will probably be very short lived. This is not to suggest that some unfavorable parental opinion justifies aborting an innovation. But it does highlight the necessity of including parental opinion in any formative evaluation of an educational innovation. The present survey of parental opinion about IPI mathematics was designed to answer questions regarding (1) the program generally, (2) pupil achievement, (3) homework, (4) pupil attitudes and behavior, (5) costs, (6) aides and volunteers, and (7) communication with the school. Each of these issues touches on important aspects of IPI.

Twenty-eight interviews were conducted with parents from School B and E using an interview schedule and guide adopted from the Alberta study (Oliva et al., 1971). This sample constitutes about 7 percent of the parents at those schools who have children in the IPI program. A stratified random sampling procedure was used, making certain that equal numbers of parents from both schools and each grade were included. These stratifications were introduced to ensure that any systematic program differences with regard to school and grade level would be reflected in the data.

All interviewees consented to be interviewed after being contacted initially by the principals of the two schools involved. The principal of School B contacted the parents by telephone; the principal of School E, by letter. All of the interviewees selected prior to contact agreed to be interviewed. After this initial contact, each interviewee was contacted by the interviewer to arrange a time convenient to the interviewee for a 45-minute (approximately) session. In each case, the interviewee was given the option of being interviewed in his home or in the office of the interviewer. All chose their own home. The same interviewer, a trained sociologist and young mother herself, conducted and taped all interviews. Four pilot interviews were conducted prior to the study, and the tape recordings were evaluated and discussed in detail by the interviewer and principal investigators together in order to enhance data reliability.

Results
Data concerning general parental attitudes toward IPI indicate a far greater frequency of positive over negative comments. The positive comments centered around individualization of rate of student progress and urged the use of similar approaches in other subject areas. Some concern was expressed over the problems of the child who moves to a non-IPI school or is promoted out of the grades in which the program is offered. The latter issue underlines an impression, not uncommon, that the traditional lockstep approach to instruction actually results in all members of a class or grade progressing to the same point. The disparity in achievement among members of a given class has always been very great, but traditional approaches deny its existence. IPI measures this disparity and attempts to exploit it to the advantage of the individual student. Most negative comments made about the program in general seemed to result from confusion or little knowledge about IPI on the part of parents. Several interviewees, in fact, complained that the principal ought to have explained the program in a home-and-school or parent–teacher meeting. Both principals had done this a number of times and had given considerable prior publicity to each session. A few negative comments, however, opposed educational innovation generally, and one parent felt that her "highstrung" daughter was frustrated by having to wait for prescriptions in class.

    Data on parental attitudes toward pupil achievement indicate that the frequency of positive comments substantially surpasses the frequency of negative comments. For the most part, positive reactions focused on the advantages of being able to work at the student's own rate. This was seen as resulting in greater speed of learning or better understanding of the material covered. One mother commented, for example, that "she [her daughter] is only working at the grade three level, but she is learning what she is doing this year." Again, negative attitudes toward IPI seemed to be due to lack of information about the program, although one parent objected to allowing her child to be left behind by those who were learning faster. Another felt that children needed to be pushed and that enabling them to move at their own rate was simply inviting student inactivity.

    Parental opinions of the lack of student homework in IPI mathematics were evenly split. Those who objected cited the need to get used to homework for later grades, remedying difficulties with parents' help, and supplementing drill activities. An impression left with the evaluator was that most parents who objected to no homework were disappointed about not being more involved in and knowledgeable about their child's education. Helping with homework enables them to gain some notion of the school's programs. Perhaps schools should consider the role of homework as a form of program feedback to the community through parents before deciding to accept or reject it.

In the opinion of most parents, their child's attitude toward mathematics was very good, but this had been the case before IPI (20 parents expressed this opinion). Seven parents said that their children were much more interested in math now and felt that IPI had increased their sense of self-responsibility. Several parents were of the opinion that their children disliked math very much but indicated that this had also been the case before IPI. One parent preferred the old program.

Of the 28 parents asked if they would be willing to pay an extra ten dollars a year for IPI if that became necessary, 5 indicated that they did not think it was worth the cost, 8 required more information before making that decision, and 15 said that they would pay ten dollars a year for its support. Of these 15, 10 stipulated that their support was contingent upon improved pupil performance over the traditional mathematics program. These data probably should be interpreted as favorable toward IPI. The 18 responses requiring further information or proof of improved student performance, however, point to the importance of the school's methods of communication with parents, about which parents seem to feel mildly satisfied. Twenty-one parents felt that there had been no change in interaction with the teacher, and 17 no change with the principal, since the IPI program began. Although schools B and E have tried to improve communications with the community since IPI began, the task is a difficult one, sometimes because of unrealistic parental expectations about the responsibility for taking initiative in the matter. One parent, for example, was dissatisfied with the amount of interaction she had had with her child's teacher; the teacher, however, had arranged an interview that the parent did not attend, and the latter clearly expected the teacher to make further contact. It should also be noted that the majority of parental opinion about school communication was positive, perhaps indicating that although parents sometimes wish they knew more about the school (especially when being interviewed), the amount of time and effort they in fact devoted to acquiring that information was about all that they were prepared to spend. A possible explanation of these data is that Schools B and E were already at a high level of interaction with regard to community communication before IPI, so that increasing efforts now produce diminishing returns.

Parental opinions about the use of paid teacher aides and volunteers in schools B and E was split. Once again, negative comments seemed to be generated largely by lack of information as to the assistants' tasks. Concern was expressed, by both those who reacted negatively and those who responded positively, about the danger of using untrained assistants to do the teacher's job. Those who reacted negatively also gave as reasons unnecessary additional costs for aides, the possibility that volunteers were taking jobs from teachers, and the fact that teachers have too little to do already without being given more help. Probably the most useful formative comment for schools B and E involved dissatisfaction among volunteer parents, who in some cases were doing the same job that the aides were being paid to do. Some prior clarification of roles would probably help to alleviate this source of contention.

A major finding of this portion of the evaluation was the very small amount of information parents had regarding the IPI program. The value of attempting to supplement that information, although the task is probably an onerous one, is evidenced by the fact that by far the majority of negative opinions held by parents about IPI were due to lack of information or misinformation. Similarly, many parents generally favoring the program (and they did constitute the majority) demonstrated greater knowledge about it. This is not to suggest, however, that all parents who favored IPI knew what they were endorsing. Certainly, the transcripts indicate that several respondents viewed the school as an institution whose actions were above judgment and for this reason would approve of almost any reasonable action it chose to take. This situation modifies the apparent proportion of favorable opinion and reinforces the need for increased school–parent communication, even if the information passing over that communication channel travels almost exclusively in one direction for some time. Perhaps an increase in the parent-volunteer programs is the most readily available means of improving such communication.

In the final analysis, the success of the IPI mathematics program is dependent upon student achievement. The data presented here suggest that pupils in schools B and E did advance substantially in mathematics skill during the program. As has been pointed out, however, the magnitude of their gains in relation to gains that might have been made in another program has yet to be assessed and is not a simple comparison to make. Whether or not the comparison is to be a favorable one for IPI depends as much on the instruments used in the evaluation as on the effect of the program. Assuming that IPI objectives are considered acceptable by the school persons concerned, IPI instruments probably should be relied upon most heavily in such an evaluation.

Given the tentative appearance of substantial student achievement, the program at present may be considered a reasonable success on the basis of the highly positive attitude that pupils, teachers, aides, and parents have developed toward it. IPI must be unique if, as one impartial observer noted, students run in from recess hurriedly shedding hockey sticks so that they can begin their mathematics program. Undoubtedly, both attitudes and achievement are likely to improve over present levels if program implementers are able to reduce the very large amount of time spent in noninstructional pupil activity. While observation data cataloged the extent of this aspect of the program, all IPI participants were well aware of it, repeatedly citing it as the major problem to be solved.

CHAPTER 8

Toward a model for educational change and innovation

The preceding chapters of this book serve two broad purposes. First, they report in some detail a case study of organized, volitional, and validated change as it has occurred and is occurring in seventeen schools in one county in Ontario. They also serve to provide empirical data in support of a general model for educational change and innovation, the dimensions of which have been implicitly elaborated. Because we believe that the model has generalized application beyond the county in which it has been developed to date, in this chapter we will explicate its dimensions and discuss their interaction in some detail. Hopefully, this discussion will at least begin to make this particular diffusion model applicable to other educational regions.

The model for diffusing educational change and innovation has seven major components. These include:

1. Marriage of the frequently disparate school and academic worlds
2. Generation of a climate for change
3. Uses of evaluation in three specific roles
4. Curriculum development strategies
5. Interschool cooperation
6. County-wide communication networks
7. Teacher responsibility for change

ACADEMIC–SCHOOL INTERACTION

Inextricably woven into the intentions of this model is the operational position of the TVC with regard to the role in educational change of academia generally and of regional field centers and laboratories in particular. This position needs to be briefly clarified. The TVC is part of the Ontario Institute for Studies in Education and the Department of Educational Theory of the University of Toronto; as such, its primary business is educational theory, broadly conceived. As already pointed out, educational research has thus far provided few solutions to the problems of educational practice. A major part of the blame rests on the methods whereby people concerned with research and development (R and D) work both to identify problems appropriate for their pursuit and to undertake the search for solutions. In too many instances, problems are identified by R and D people rather than by practitioners. Solutions to problems not identified as such by those in a position to utilize the solution are doomed prematurely in spite of potential value. The potential value of many of these solutions is questionable, however, since solutions to problems identified by the nonpractitioner must necessarily be contrived and tested under artificial conditions. One of the two major components of the Trent Valley Centre's R and D position, then, is to assist in the solution of problems identified by the educational practitioner under conditions the practitioner defines as the real world.

The complementary component of this position concerns the unique balance that the field centers must strike between the academic world and the pragmatic world of the schools. While useful solutions to real problems must be found, they must also be capable of generalization beyond the setting in which they were developed. No society is economically capable of providing support to its educational practitioners, of the quality being discussed, for the solution of problems specific to individual schools. This, in essence, is why schools within the Project work in groups, enabling external resources to be brought to bear on shared problems in an administratively and economically viable manner.

The issue of equilibrium between the worlds of theory and practice is critical for R and D work, and it is not unduly stretching the analogy to compare it with the cognitive structures and functions embedded in Piaget's theory of intellectual development. Knowledge is acquired by the invariant processes of assimilation and accommodation: assimilation by an R and D group of the components of problems in the field amenable to solution through strategies already available; and accommodation to the unique elements within each of these problems that require knowledge generation or schematic resynthesis in order to arrive at a higher level or a more appropriate solution. Basic to Piaget's theory of intellectual development and similarly to the Trent Valley Centre's R and D position is the necessity for the learner to interact with the environment in a two-way fashion. For an R and D group merely to impose solutions to problems that it primarily identifies is to upset the balance of equilibrium so that it is heavily weighted on the side of assimilation (the organism does not accommodate to reality, but creates its own subjective reality). Piaget suggests that this type of activity is characteristic of play. On the other hand, to work only on individual school problems without intent of generalization is (for R and D persons) to accommodate too much to reality to be able to cope with it at a higher level. There is a consequent failure to assimilate those problems into existing theoretical structures capable of generating solutions with potentially wider application. Piaget characterizes this state as imitation. Neither state produces more complex cognitive structures or increasingly sophisticated solutions to educational problems from the point of view of the field center. Disequilibrium in the direction of assimilation leads only to further irrelevant educational research and development. Disequilibrium in the direction of accommodation produces useful solutions for specific schools but leaves most schools to fend for themselves.

CLIMATE FOR CHANGE   The generation of a climate for change must be considered the most critical component of change. It is also the most elusive component to describe, since it manifests itself in many ways. One tends to gain a cumulative impression of the change climate based on diverse incidents rather than a distinctive concept of high profile. One of the reasons for the low profile characterizing this climate for change is the vast amount of energy expended, because of the climate, that is not readily visible. Commitment to change carries with it responsibility for action, only a small proportion of which results in changes in classroom behavior. The visible climate and its resultant action might be considered the tip of an iceberg.

ROLES OF EVALUATION   Evaluation has been assigned three distinct roles to play in the change process: to promote, facilitate, and validate the change that takes place. Change is promoted through evaluation of present programs by stimulating thought and discussion of the status quo and providing a basis for making decisions about program adequacy with regard to current educational objectives. Change is facilitated also, since evaluative data pinpoint educational objectives not being achieved well by many students, thus providing rational criteria for deciding where change can be most profitably initiated. Considerable literature on educational change to date seems to imply that change is justified in its own right without respect to its results. Our model, however, strongly emphasizes the effectiveness of the change. Change for the sake of change is a waste of resources. Many dimensions of the innovative programs have been assessed, including attitudinal, treatment, and achievement dimensions, but the importance of specific student achievement data needs to be highlighted. Only when change produces observable, desirable differences in student outcomes can an innovation be judged as substantially better than the former program. Such a judgment of worth necessarily involves careful consideration of criterion-referenced testing and research design.

CURRICULUM DEVELOPMENT STRATEGIES

Innovative processes must result in products identifiable at some level of visibility. The strategies employed in program development in this model include four dimensions: the identification of educational objectives; the gathering or generation of materials to be used in achieving those objectives; the choice of instructional techniques for manipulating those materials in an effective manner; and evaluation of the objectives, materials, and techniques. The sorts of formative and summative evaluation required and the selection strategies exercised on materials and techniques demand that objectives be specified in operational, behavioral, or student performance terms. While many arguments have been raised against such specification, most appear amenable to solution under certain conditions (see chapter 5).

The order in which the components appear in the curriculum development process varies greatly with the needs and characteristics of the developers. In a great many instances, the shortest route to total curriculum development task completion may begin with the evaluation or materials components. Beginning with selection of materials is useful, since it quickly leads to innovations in the classroom and generates the need to move concretely into issues of objectives as a basis for decision making about selection of materials. Beginning with evaluation has the advantage of diagnosing areas of greatest present weakness and treating those areas of greatest need first. It necessarily involves beginning where one is at present and moving from this point – a very sound policy for effective change. Beginning with the objectives component is logically appropriate, but objectives specification can be a long and difficult task requiring considerable patience before the impact of such work becomes visible.

INTERSCHOOL COOPERATION AND COUNTY-WIDE COMMUNICATION NETWORK

Two networks for communication have been elaborated in the model. The first is a communication network that relates educational personnel by constituent position to one another, where the school principal is the hub of communication with respect to change and innovation. The central role of the principal in this network highlights his function as a change agent having direct communication access to senior administration, teachers, students, parents, and outside agencies (although he usually has no direct contact with elected trustees). He is therefore in a position to initiate and facilitate change in his school.

The second communication network functions as a mechanism through which the principal performs many of his facilitating activities. This network links school principals formally involved in the innovative process through cooperative groupings of various sizes, depending upon purpose. Three types of groupings are embedded in this network. The first of these is labeled a joint group and consists of all innovative school principals who wish to be a part of the change model. This group's function is to provide a forum for general issues of common concern and simple information relay. A second group, the liaison group, coordinates and facilitates the real work of the innovative schools. These schools comprise the third group, which is designed to deal with specific, substantive curriculum and other change issues. The group structure provides (1) the benefit of mutual experience; (2) the dissemination of useful information; (3) mutual support; and (4) an efficient means whereby consultative assistance (such as that provided by the Trent Valley Centre) can be mustered to deal with important problems of common concern.

TEACHER RESPONSIBILITY FOR CHANGE

While the principal is the center of the communication network, his facilitating and initiating functions are almost entirely for the purpose of giving the classroom teacher the responsibility, decision-making capability, and tools to determine what changes need to be made and how they should be undertaken. A common argument that cannot be dismissed lightly is that teachers have neither the time nor the skills to be heavily involved in curriculum development activities. While empirical evidence from this case study suggests that this is not necessarily always the case, the fact remains that the teacher's load is considerable already. Teacher responsibility for curriculum, however, does not imply that superintendents, subject-matter specialists, consultants, and trained curriculum developers cannot lighten the teachers' load greatly without violating the principle of teacher responsibility. What is suggested is that teachers should be encouraged to identify the needs they see in their classrooms, specify (at some level) the objectives they have for their students, feed other persons with information to guide the development of materials and strategies that will help meet those identified needs, and critically evaluate materials and strategies in the light of their objectives. It should be the teachers' prerogative to make the final decision of adoption, adaptation, or rejection (within the financial limitations imposed on administration), because it is the teacher who is ultimately accountable for the performance of the students exposed to the innovation.

RELATIONSHIP OF THE MODEL'S COMPONENTS

While it is important to consider these seven components in isolation, many (although certainly not all) of their features are already well known and have been part of educational knowledge for many years. The major contribution to new knowledge that this model makes concerns the dynamic ways in which the components interact to produce validated educational change. Educational literature abounds with treatises on objectives, evaluation, and communication. The school as the educational unit and teacher responsibility for goal setting were recognized many years ago by Dewey (1966). Few attempts have been made, however, to locate each component within a larger framework or strategy of change of the kind that has been discussed in this book. It is this framework that has dictated the differences in approach that are evident in the model's components.

Figure 7 illustrates how the components of this model interact, as conceptualized to date, through seven temporally sequenced stages from initial agreement to change to the stage of field trials of new programs. The latter two stages are as yet not clearly defined, and they represent a future focus of research. It should also be noted that some of the elements and orders within each of the other stages will undoubtedly alter as work progresses to refine the model. The model began, in fact, as a model *of* change, and refinement is in the direction of making it a model *for* change. In the remainder of this chapter, the stage-based component interactions will be discussed, although briefly, since each has been mentioned already in the context of the case study report.

Stage 1: Agreements to Begin
This stage begins with a decision at the county level on the part of a number of practitioners (a) that their schools could be better and that they are prepared to investigate how such improvement could be pursued. Once this decision has been made, the agreement to begin in a formal manner (f) necessitates gaining the cooperation of all affected groups, including principals, teachers, administrators, consultants, and R and D persons who may be able to facilitate the desired change. This gaining of cooperation is the purpose of meetings (b), (c), (d), and (e). The result of these meetings and formal agreement to begin is the planning of an advisory committee (g) that has a broad educational community base and is designed as a sounding board for the innovators to test their means and ends before and during their operationalization. Basic to decisions made at this stage are the concepts of teacher responsibility and the school as the critical educational unit.

Stage 2: Establish Organization
The establishment of an organization for change begins with (a) a selection of schools. Two of the most important issues here are who does the selection and what are the selection criteria. The preferred situation usually involves school self-selection on the basis of evinced interest in change. When this is the case, the process moves directly to school-level meetings (b) with and among teachers, principals, and anyone else who the school unit feels would be helpful – possibly R and D personnel and/or consultants. From this point, two routes are possible, leading to the teachers' study of the change process in released time (f). One of these routes involves the principal's studying the change process first (d) as a means of determining

techniques for initiating an interest in his teachers. This route would be followed if there were no strong initial pressure to change from the teaching body. In such an instance, part of this study might lead the principal to plan for the use of expert and volunteer manpower (g) as a way of stimulating interest. An alternate route, appropriate when the principal is ready to change and when he knows that teachers also are ready, is to select the teachers who will begin (e) and initiate their study of the change process, perhaps in cooperation with him. Teacher selection again is a critical issue, and self-selection is vital where possible. The task of change is a massive one, however, and for an entire, larger staff to be involved simultaneously at the outset would present problems that might be insurmountable.

Where self-selection does not occur, the route from (a) to (d) involves a meeting or meetings of principals, administrators, and R and D consultants (c) in order to facilitate selection. The gathering of sociometric data has been contemplated (but thus far not employed) for assisting in such selection. Two points must be made clear here. First, the reaching of the "go or no-go" decision point with regard to change after a study of process is most fundamentally the reaching of a point where the teacher's decision takes priority. Second, there are two possible routes if the "no-go" decision is made. One of these routes is to return to further study of the change process. The second route is to drop out of involvement in change altogether, a difficult or impossible action to take.

Stage 3: Problem and Goal Selection
The decision to proceed with change leads to a study of general school goals on the part of the teacher (a), initially at a high level of generality but at increasingly specific levels as study proceeds. The result of this stage is either the generation and/or selection of specific program goals by the teacher or the selection of programs that speak to general teacher goals. In order to reach this stage, teachers must, and principals probably should, be involved in studying the technology of goal statements in student performance terms and studying available programs that potentially achieve these teacher-generated objectives (c) and (d). The school community also might be involved (e) at a general level, in order to ensure that the broad goals of the school reflect the goals of its most relevant society. Depending upon whether or not a ready-made program can be found or a new teacher-generated program is to be developed, two routes into stage 4 are possible.

Stage 4: Study Available Solutions
The route from stage 3 (g) is to stage 4 (a), the selection of the innovative program, and this route can be a reasonably swift one, involving the principal's search for

authority to proceed and then teacher training and study of the program leading directly to a pilot trial at stage 5. If the innovators enter stage 4 at point (b), they must examine available materials, select appropriate parts of them, organize these parts, and write auxiliary materials (e), (f), and (h). They must also design the instructional techniques to be used with these materials (g). They then are able to move into stage 5 at the same level apparently as those who choose the other route. This equality of stages may be misleading, however, since those who take the route (b) to (h) may need to recycle through stage 4 several times. If preselection criteria are adequate, this is less likely for those who choose the (a) to (d) route.

Stage 5: Pilot Trial
At this stage the design of pilot trials using an appropriate evaluation design (a), pretest (b), trial initiation (c), and the gathering of formative evaluation data (d) are common steps, but alternate routes become available after this point. The choice of route is based on results of the formative evaluation, and the possible routes involve program adoption, adaptation, or rejection. If the data suggest adoption (e), the route is directly into stage 6. An adaptation decision (f) may suggest merely the beginning of another trial with minor alterations or as large a step as moving back to stage 4. The rejection decision (g) takes the innovator back to program or goal selection in stage 3.

Stage 6: Adopt, Adapt, or Reject
A decision to adopt at stage 5 leads to stage 6, the recycling of the innovative program within the innovative school (a) and the gathering of additional evaluation data (b). On the basis of these data, adopt, adapt, or reject decisions (c), (d), and (e) are once again possible. A decision to adopt leads to the reporting to other interested schools of the results of evaluation (f), and such data then are considered to be used in the summative mode. This report of data may lead to plans for program field trials (g) in other schools that are at point (f) in stage 3. A decision to adapt, depending upon the extent of adaptation required, may lead back to any point in stage 4, and even back to (h) in stage 3 if problems are very fundamental. A decision to reject may lead out of the change process.

Stage 7: Field Trial
The steps in stage 7 are not clear at this time and probably will not be until Project programs reach this stage – a stage only one program has entered to date. It appears, however, that designs for evaluation and diffusion (a) and (b) are integral parts of this stage, as is a carefully planned evaluation of this diffusion model (c).

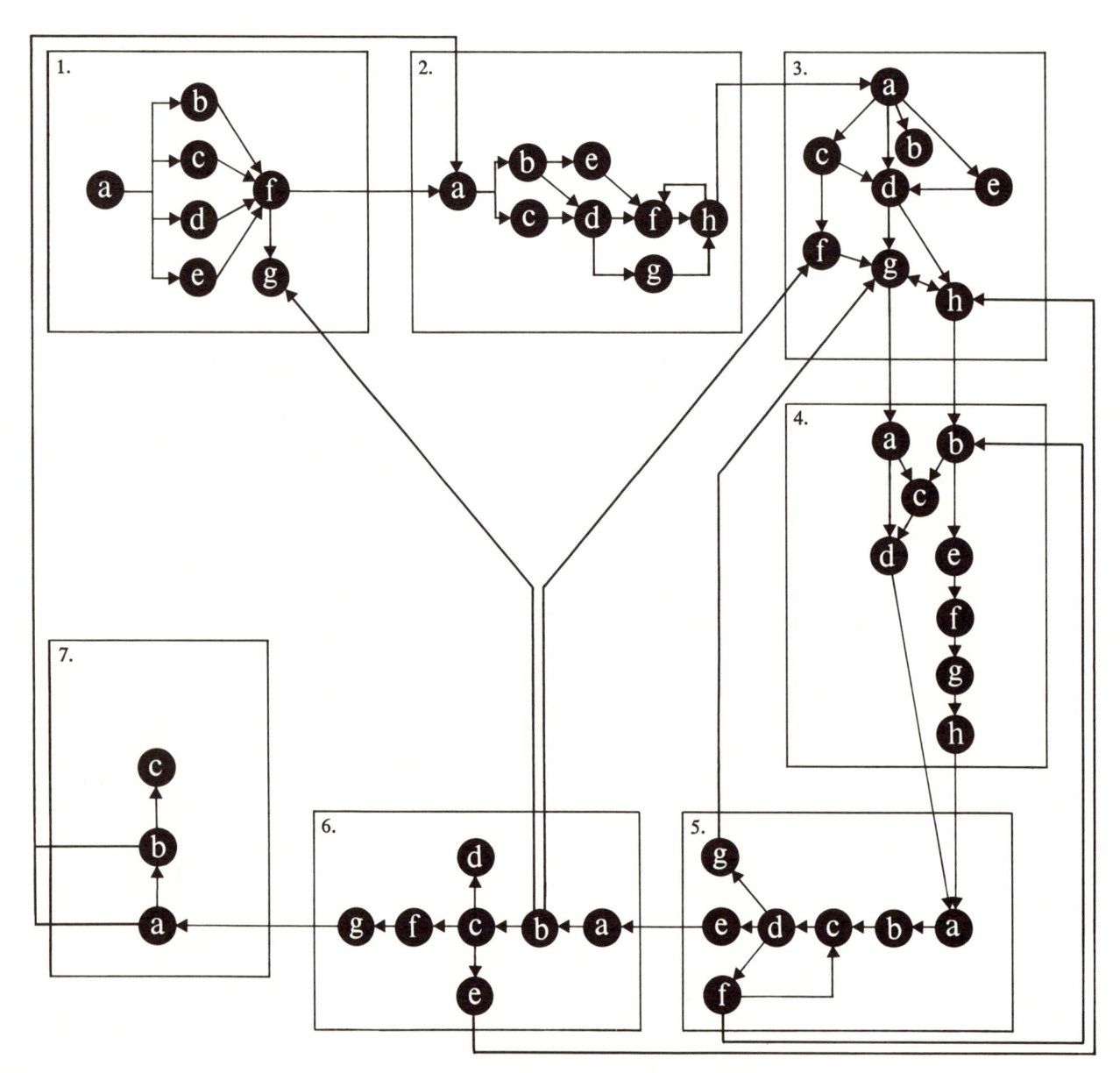

Figure 7. School change model: interaction of components.

KEY TO FIGURE 7

1. **Agreements to begin**
   a. Meeting of representatives
   b. Meeting of principal and teacher representatives
   c. Meeting of Research and Development (R & D)
   d. Meeting of consultants
   e. Meeting of other manpower groups
   f. Specific agreement to proceed
   g. Plan advisory committee

2. **Establish organization**
   a. Select schools
   b. School-level meetings: teachers and principal
   c. Meeting of principal, administration, R & D consultants
   d. Principal studies change process
   e. Select teachers within schools
   f. Teachers study change process within school during released time
   g. Principal plans use of expert and volunteer manpower
   h. Teachers make go or no-go decision

3. **Problem and goal selection**
   a. Teachers study general school goals
   b. Principal acts as facilitator
   c. Principal studies behavioral goal specification
   d. Teachers study behavioral goal specification
   e. School community interacts on general goals
   f. Principal studies available solutions (consultants)
   g. Teachers study available solutions (consultants)
   h. Teachers generate or select instructional goals

4. **Study available solutions**
   a. Teachers select innovative program
   b. Teachers decide to develop innovative program
   c. Principal seeks authority to proceed
   d. Teacher training and study
   e. Teachers study materials available
   f. Teachers select materials and organize
   g. Teachers develop or select instructional objective
   h. Teachers prepare auxiliary material

5. **Pilot trial**
   a. Design pilot trial (time sequence)
   b. Pretest
   c. Begin trials
   d. Formative evaluation
   e. Adopt decision ⎫
   f. Adapt   ⎬ Module
   g. Reject   ⎭

6. **Adopt, adapt, or reject**
   a. Recycle program within school
   b. Report evaluation data for program
   c. Adopt
   d. Adapt
   e. Reject
   f. Report summative evaluation data
   g. Plan field trial

7. **Field trial**
   a. Design for evaluation
   b. Design for diffusion
   c. Plan evaluation of diffusion model

CONCLUSION Future development, refinement, and evaluation of the model may well take the form of systematic hypothesis testing in relation to components multiplied by stage interaction. The model may be conceptualized as a matrix with 49 cells (see figure 8), not all of which are filled. Those that are filled, however, suggest reasonably unique development problems (many of which are unsolved), lending themselves to scientific investigation potentially resulting in solutions to a number of problems of critical concern to educators.

Figure 8 illustrates the total possible number of presently available interactions, and more may appear with further development. Each cell may also be viewed as a matrix itself with a varying number of cells in need of study.

As this book reflects, the process of change is not easily analyzed. Robert Stake (1972) has suggested that theories, test scores, statistical processes, and many other tools of the educational researcher are simplifiers, "simple representations of the complex." They help us by reducing complex phenomena to entities we are able to understand and come to grips with, but they also mislead us by suggesting that the phenomena being studied are more limited than they really are.

Analysis of the change process has often been dichotomized for purposes of

Stages	Climate for change	Academic–school interaction	Evaluation	Curriculum development	Interschool cooperation	Communication network	Teacher responsibility
1. Agree to begin							
2. Establish organization							
3. Select problems and goals							
4. Study available solutions							
5. Pilot trials							
6. Adopt, adapt, reject							
7. Field trials							

Figure 8. Change model as a matrix suggesting potential areas for hypothesis testing.

simplification. One set of theories focuses on the individual as the center of change, ignoring the system within which he operates. Systems analysis, in contrast, tends to place organizational norms in a superordinate position with respect to effecting change. Our own position is that educational change needs to be recognized for the complex process that it is. Perhaps one of the most fruitful ways of building a change theory that has significant power is to derive a tentative model that allows for complex interactions such as those discussed in this chapter, and to build upon, modify, and elaborate this model in the process of involvement in change that really is occurring in the educational community. The simplicity of many so-called change theories severely limits their value.

Appendix

Table 1 / School C Math, Grades 4–6, 1970/71:
Means and Standard Deviations

	CRM pretest			CRM posttest			CRM gain		
	N	Mean	SD	N	Mean	SD [a]	N	Mean	SD [a]
Grade 4									
Class 1	25	150.56	25.77	24	179.21	17.55	24	28.65	14.73
Class 2	21	141.00	28.98	23	171.26	25.53	20	30.26	17.92
Grade 5									
Class 1	27	134.16	35.31	2	158.00	—	[b]	23.84	—
Class 2	24	122.50	27.51	2	183.00	—	[b]	60.50	—
Grade 6									
Class 1	23	65.46	16.54	2	95.00	—	[b]	29.54	—
Class 2	23	79.90	20.95	2	113.50	—	[b]	33.60	—
Grand mean		112.47			150.00			37.53	

[a] Standard deviations could not be calculated in cases where the data base was extremely low and randomization procedures were used.

[b] See p. 80 for a description of the calculation of gain scores. In view of the randomization procedures used, no N is given for grades 5 and 6.

Table 2 / School C Math, Grade 4, 1970/71:
Means and Standard Deviations, by Skill Area

	\multicolumn{3}{c	}{**CRM pretest**}	\multicolumn{3}{c	}{**CRM posttest**}	**CRM gain**
	N	Mean	SD	N	Mean	SD	
Addition							
Class 1	26	60.04	5.98	26	61.04	4.56	1.00
Class 2	24	55.42	6.32	23	56.83	6.34	1.41
Subtraction							
Class 1	36	36.00	5.08	26	40.19	2.59	4.19
Class 2	23	35.87	5.86	22	38.55	3.91	2.68
Multiplication							
Class 1	26	36.15	11.08	26	49.35	5.84	13.20
Class 2	23	31.78	14.68	22	46.36	9.15	14.58
Division							
Class 1	26	15.42	5.89	26	23.92	5.10	8.50
Class 2	23	15.22	6.72	22	23.05	7.88	7.83
Problem-solving							
Class 1	25	2.80	2.14	24	5.25	1.96	2.45
Class 2	22	3.50	2.06	23	5.48	2.86	1.98
Total							
Class 1	25	150.56	25.77	24	179.21	17.55	28.65
Class 2	21	141.00	28.98	23	171.26	25.43	30.26

Table 3 / School C Math, Grade 5, 1970/71:
Means and Standard Deviations, by Skill Area

	CRM pretest N	CRM pretest Mean	CRM pretest SD	CRM posttest[a] N	CRM posttest[a] Mean	CRM gain
Addition						
Class 1	26	9.73	0.53	2	10.00	0.27
Class 2	27	8.11	1.97	2	7.50	−0.61
Subtraction						
Class 1	26	5.31	1.16	2	5.50	0.19
Class 2	27	4.67	1.21	2	4.00	−0.67
Multiplication						
Class 1	26	17.19	3.92	2	20.50	3.31
Class 2	27	14.78	5.14	2	13.00	−1.78
Division						
Class 1	26	11.16	4.25	2	16.00	4.84
Class 2	27	9.41	4.74	2	17.00	7.59
Fractions						
Class 1	26	27.27	7.25	2	40.00	12.73
Class 2	27	30.37	9.21	2	34.50	4.13
Decimals						
Class 1	26	8.85	4.23	2	13.50	4.65
Class 2	27	21.93	5.96	2	13.50	−8.43
Percent						
Class 1	26	1.92	3.57	2	27.00	25.08
Class 2	27	5.85	3.88	2	21.50	15.65
Ratio						
Class 1	25	3.44	3.04	2	6.50	3.06
Class 2	26	5.58	2.32	2	7.00	1.42
Linear measurement						
Class 1	25	9.44	1.89	2	11.00	1.56
Class 2	26	9.08	1.96	2	8.00	−1.08
Area measurement						
Class 1	25	1.92	2.08	2	3.00	1.08
Class 2	26	2.38	2.40	2	2.50	0.12
Volume measurement						
Class 1	25	1.44	0.82	2	2.00	0.56
Class 2	26	1.62	0.64	2	1.50	−0.12

Table 3 – *continued*

	CRM pretest			CRM posttest[a]		CRM gain
	N	Mean	SD	N	Mean	
Money						
Class 1	25	2.92	1.00	2	4.00	1.08
Class 2	26	2.77	1.14	2	3.50	0.73
Time						
Class 1	25	13.24	3.36	2	15.00	1.76
Class 2	26	13.65	3.35	2	14.50	0.85
Graphing						
Class 1	26	4.31	1.07	2	3.50	−0.81
Class 2	0	—	—	0	—	—
Problem-solving						
Class 1	25	4.36	1.44	2	5.50	1.14
Class 2	27	3.96	1.45	2	5.00	1.04
Total						
Class 1	25	122.50	27.51	2	183.00	60.50
Class 2	26	134.16	35.31	2	153.00	18.84

[a] Standard deviations could not be calculated for posttest scores in view of the low data base and the randomization procedures used.

Table 4 / School C Math, Grade 6, 1970/71:
Means and Standard Deviations, by Skill Area

	\multicolumn{3}{c}{CRM pretest}	\multicolumn{2}{c}{CRM posttest [a]}	CRM gain
	N	Mean	SD	N	Mean	
Whole numbers						
Class 1	25	7.36	2.10	2	11.50	4.14
Class 2	25	8.92	2.87	2	11.50	2.58
Fractions						
Class 1	25	12.08	7.26	2	25.00	12.92
Class 2	25	25.80	10.06	2	33.00	7.20
Decimals						
Class 1	24	15.33	3.62	2	23.50	8.17
Class 2	25	15.20	4.83	2	24.50	9.30
Percent						
Class 1	24	12.29	3.83	2	13.00	0.71
Class 2	25	12.40	5.02	2	15.00	2.60
Ratio						
Class 1	23	9.87	3.52	2	11.00	1.13
Class 2	25	7.64	3.87	2	11.00	3.36
Linear measurement						
Class 1	24	2.96	1.52	2	6.00	3.04
Class 2	25	2.60	2.02	2	7.50	4.90
Area measurement						
Class 1	24	1.96	0.69	2	1.00	−0.96
Class 2	25	1.60	0.65	2	4.00	2.40
Volume measurement						
Class 1	24	2.13	0.99	2	1.50	−0.63
Class 2	25	1.52	1.23	2	2.50	0.98
Weight measurement						
Class 1	23	0.48	0.59	2	1.00	0.52
Class 2	25	1.96	0.20	2	2.00	0.04
Problem-solving						
Class 1	23	1.00	0.74	2	1.50	0.50
Class 2	23	2.26	0.54	2	2.50	0.24
Total						
Class 1	23	65.46	16.54	2	95.00	29.54
Class 2	23	79.90	20.95	2	113.50	33.60

[a] Standard deviations could not be calculated for posttest scores in view of the low data base and the randomization procedures used.

Table 5 / School C Math, Grade 4, 1970/71:
Correlations on Main Variables

	(2) SES r	(2) SES N	(3) IQ r	(3) IQ N	(4) CTBS concepts r	(4) CTBS concepts N	(5) CTBS problems r	(5) CTBS problems N	(6) CTBS total r	(6) CTBS total N	(7) CRM pretest r	(7) CRM pretest N	(8) CRM posttest r	(8) CRM posttest N	(9) CRM gain r	(9) CRM gain N
(1) Sex																
Class 1	.30	25	−.06	26	.02	24	−.15	23	−.07	24	−.12	25	−.15	25	.01	24
Class 2	−.18	24	.03	23	.00	3	.00	3	.00	3	.37	20	.39	23	.10	20
Combined	.07	49	−.02	49	−.05	27	−.22	26	−.15	27	.11	45	.15	48	.06	44
(2) SES																
Class 1			.44	25	.35	23	.16	22	.32	23	.43	24	.52	24	−.10	23
Class 2			.28	23	.89	3	.99	3	.96	3	−.01	20	.03	23	.05	20
Combined			.38	48	.35	26	.19	25	.32	26	.22	44	.25	47	−.03	43
(3) IQ																
Class 1					.69	24	.43	23	.65	24	.44	25	.54	25	−.11	24
Class 2					.66	3	.87	3	.80	3	.61	20	.57	23	−.18	20
Combined					.70	27	.46	26	.65	27	.51	45	.54	48	−.14	44
(4) CTBS concepts																
Class 1							.62	23	.90	24	.69	23	.63	24	−.46	23
Class 2							.94	3	.98	3	−1.00	2	.87	3	1.00	2
Combined							.66	26	.91	27	.68	25	.66	27	−.44	25
(5) CTBS problems																
Class 1									.88	23	.57	22	.58	23	−.28	22
Class 2									.99	3	−1.00	2	.66	3	1.00	2
Combined									.90	26	.52	24	.63	26	−.23	24
(6) CTBS total																
Class 1											.70	23	.65	24	−.44	23
Class 2											−1.00	2	.76	3	1.00	2
Combined											.67	25	.69	27	−.41	25
(7) CRM pretest																
Class 1													.84	24	−.77	24
Class 2													.78	20	−.54	20
Combined													.81	44	−.65	44
(8) CRM posttest																
Class 1															−.29	24
Class 2															.10	20
Combined															−.08	24

Table 6 / School A Social Studies, Grades 4–6, 1970/71:
Means and Standard Deviations on Main Variables

	SES N	SES Mean	SES SD	IQ N	IQ Mean	IQ SD	CRM pretest N	CRM pretest Mean	CRM pretest SD	CRM posttest N	CRM posttest Mean	CRM posttest SD	CRM gain N	CRM gain Mean	CRM gain SD
Grade 4															
Class 1	30	52.25	16.60	30	94.33	16.92	28	21.46	9.32	26	27.19	8.71	26	5.73	6.71
Class 2	25	49.64	19.36	20	100.15	14.17	26	13.88	4.14	26	12.12	4.95	22	−1.76	3.90
Grade 5															
Class 1	33	52.04	18.94	32	99.72	18.84	35	22.91	8.68	34	25.59	7.80	32	2.78	4.66
Class 2	30	49.93	18.27	29	99.07	15.79	30	23.53	6.68	29	20.24	6.02	28	−3.82	5.28
Grade 6															
Class 1	27	52.87	16.56	28	110.96	16.10	30	26.97	6.31	30	26.23	5.89	26	−0.81	6.16
Grade 4															
Males	29	47.21	16.44	25	92.20	15.25	29	16.24	8.34	28	17.54	10.00	28	1.57	6.86
Females	26	55.36	18.58	25	101.12	15.74	25	19.64	7.69	24	22.13	10.19	20	3.90	6.99
Grade 5															
Males	30	51.43	18.12	29	95.90	17.92	32	21.06	7.44	31	19.94	6.99	29	−1.52	6.77
Females	33	50.68	19.12	32	102.59	16.39	33	25.27	7.63	32	26.22	6.68	31	0.84	4.80
Grade 6															
Males	12	54.41	18.05	16	107.81	15.97	16	23.88	5.60	16	24.19	6.25	15	0.33	4.06
Females	15	51.63	15.17	12	115.17	15.30	14	30.50	5.11	14	28.57	4.40	11	−2.36	7.93
All students	145	51.39	18.03	139	100.75	17.53	149	22.01	8.44	145	22.52	8.72	134	0.62	6.55

[a] This column contains the average gain score of all individuals who completed both pretest and posttest. The average gain calculated by subtracting the mean pretest score from the mean posttest score differs slightly.

Table 7 / Conceptual Skills, 1970/71:
Case Study Group Means and Standard Deviations on Main Variables, by SES Level

	SES Mean	SES SD	IQ Mean	IQ SD	CRM pretest Mean	CRM pretest SD	CRM posttest Mean	CRM posttest SD	CRM gain Mean	CRM gain SD
High E (N = 20)	61.90	15.02	126.15	18.80	138.30	16.00	165.45	8.96	27.15	10.37
Low E (N = 15)	37.83	11.35	116.93	8.77	132.07	11.84	163.87	13.55	31.80	15.92
Low C (N = 14)	47.99	20.25	116.86	17.54	140.79	16.74	151.50	18.16	10.71	18.68
High C (N = 20)	55.26	16.50	116.65	15.15	141.15	16.53	155.00	16.08	13.85	17.11

Table 8 / Conceptual Skills, 1970/71:
Analysis of Variance of CRM Posttest Scores

	Degrees of freedom	Mean	F ratio	p
SES	1	0.16	0.07	
Treatment	1	24.32	10.50	< .01
Interaction	1	0.17	0.07	
Error	71	2.32		

Table 9 / Conceptual Skills, 1970/71:
Case Study Group Means on CRM Posttest Scores

	Treatment N	Treatment Mean	Control N	Control Mean
High SES	20	165.50	20	155.00
Low SES	18	165.50	17	153.11

Table 10 / Conceptual Skills, 1970/71:
Correlations for Case Study Groups Using Within-group Data

	(2) SES	(3) IQ	(4) CRM pretest	(5) CRM posttest	(6) CRM gain
(1) Sex					
High E (N = 20)	−.20	−.13	.07	.16	.04
Low E (N = 15)	−.11	−.26	.10	.13	.04
Low C (N = 14)	−.36	−.42	−.24	−.26	−.03
High C (N = 20)	−.15	.00	.50	−.09	−.57
(2) SES					
High E		−.05	.19	.09	−.21
Low E		.08	−.10	.00	.07
Low C		.74	.42	.35	−.04
High C		.25	.02	−.11	−.12
(3) IQ					
High E			.41	.55	−.15
Low E			.32	.13	−.13
Low C			.41	.66	.28
High C			.53	.37	−.16
(4) CRM pretest					
High E				.80	−.85
Low E				.22	−.56
Low C				.43	−.48
High C				.45	−.54
(5) CRM posttest					
High E					−.37
Low E					.69
Low C					.59
High C					.51

Table 11 / Conceptual Skills, 1970/71:
Means and Standard Deviations on Main Variables

	\multicolumn{3}{c	}{CRM pretest}	\multicolumn{3}{c	}{CRM posttest}	\multicolumn{3}{c	}{CRM gain}
	N	Mean	SD	N	Mean	SD	N	Mean	SD
School I	42	124.10	20.06	39	161.10	13.03	39	36.18	15.72
School A	6	134.00	17.98	6	165.00	8.94	6	31.00	16.11
School H	12	177.33	7.40	11	172.55	5.47	11	−3.91	6.24
School G	35	127.14	21.68	32	151.50	26.41	30	26.80	16.77
School F	43	144.37	24.85	40	166.73	15.59	39	24.13	18.71
School C	43	130.91	19.89	43	160.79	14.99	43	29.88	17.55
School D	45	125.96	22.38	44	160.77	18.30	44	36.70	23.12
Males	105	132.31	23.45	101	161.00	20.14	100	29.65	18.61
Females	121	133.93	25.75	114	161.54	15.85	112	28.88	21.85
All students	226	133.18	24.72	215	161.28	18.00	212	29.24	20.39

Table 12 / IPI Mathematics, Grades 4–6, 1970/71:
Means and Standard Deviations on Main Variables

	SES N	SES Mean	SES SD	IQ N	IQ Mean	IQ SD	CRM pretest N	CRM pretest Mean	CRM pretest SD	CRM posttest N	CRM posttest Mean	CRM posttest SD
Grade 4												
SCHOOL A												
Class 1	31	41.47	13.21	31	90.74	13.38	32	46.38	22.64	32	90.16	41.29
Class 2	29	38.72	12.53	30	98.43	14.23	30	58.67	18.33	30	106.90	30.04
SCHOOL E												
Class 1	25	47.16	15.43	26	97.15	14.07	27	54.00	17.26	27	103.81	32.50
Class 2	24	42.39	13.15	24	98.67	10.76	26	58.62	13.95	26	109.54	25.96
Grade 5												
SCHOOL A												
Class 1	31	40.73	13.20	32	96.84	13.07	32	67.38	22.89	32	111.53	33.54
Class 2	29	42.98	14.76	32	100.75	13.87	32	70.25	26.43	32	116.06	33.93
SCHOOL E												
Class 1	29	38.94	10.81	29	95.34	11.05	29	59.07	12.85	29	107.90	24.77
Class 2	29	39.99	11.54	30	96.60	15.74	31	55.45	14.66	31	92.97	25.89
Class 3	30	44.85	12.45	29	95.31	10.34	31	56.68	12.79	31	106.16	22.93
Grade 6												
SCHOOL A												
Class 1	29	43.12	14.04	29	102.10	15.32	29	95.72	43.02	29	144.10	51.63
Class 2	29	36.26	11.00	23	96.52	12.71	29	95.79	38.20	29	142.72	46.91
SCHOOL E												
Class 1	31	43.06	11.84	30	97.63	12.52	31	65.65	16.91	31	119.35	32.82
Class 2	31	42.05	12.86	30	93.87	14.28	29	63.69	18.65	29	125.17	28.39
Grade 4												
Males	62	41.95	13.31	63	94.22	14.52	66	54.64	20.18	66	103.80	36.08
Females	47	42.64	14.61	48	98.42	12.09	49	53.47	17.92	49	99.84	31.32
Grade 5												
Males	73	41.13	12.98	77	96.73	15.37	79	64.29	22.62	79	108.66	33.28
Females	75	41.88	12.64	75	97.36	10.40	76	59.39	16.16	76	105.28	25.45
Grade 6												
Males	60	42.54	13.35	54	94.35	16.25	60	85.85	41.05	60	139.80	49.90
Females	60	39.81	12.07	58	100.53	11.02	58	73.88	25.63	58	125.17	31.08
All students	377	41.61	13.14	375	96.90	13.62	388	65.09	27.28	388	113.34	37.58

CRM gain			CTBS concepts			CTBS problems			CTBS total		
N	Mean	SD	N	Mean	SD	N	Mean	SD	N	Mean	SD
32	43.97	19.86	32	32.34	25.29	32	27.75	20.56	32	28.13	23.52
30	48.47	13.91	30	39.00	28.01	30	38.90	23.16	30	38.43	25.76
27	49.81	18.45	27	41.89	27.86	27	40.33	20.37	27	41.22	25.82
26	50.92	14.81	24	52.75	27.57	24	50.38	28.59	24	51.58	27.87
32	44.16	16.53	32	26.78	23.13	32	36.28	25.06	32	29.03	24.22
32	45.82	12.36	32	44.22	27.97	32	45.22	24.97	32	44.06	27.16
29	48.83	15.74	28	36.07	25.17	28	31.89	21.87	26	31.62	24.61
31	37.52	12.85	30	49.57	28.47	30	42.00	27.19	27	46.67	30.60
31	49.52	13.29	30	42.40	24.71	30	43.23	25.43	28	42.39	25.55
29	48.38	19.42	27	63.44	11.54	27	60.48	13.76	27	37.74	12.62
29	46.93	13.31	29	56.69	10.57	29	56.45	10.60	29	30.48	8.83
31	53.77	20.53	29	52.31	23.49	29	39.41	21.87	20	41.65	25.34
29	61.83	14.99	28	52.86	21.15	28	45.89	24.67	23	51.00	21.99
66	49.26	18.17	64	37.83	29.08	64	36.47	25.66	64	36.16	28.19
49	46.51	15.76	49	44.51	26.22	49	41.20	22.52	49	42.65	24.72
79	44.37	15.45	76	40.82	29.04	76	39.92	27.18	72	39.56	29.56
76	45.89	14.19	76	38.67	25.07	76	39.79	23.63	73	37.81	25.10
60	54.12	19.03	55	54.98	20.33	55	51.56	21.48	51	38.35	19.31
58	51.33	17.45	58	57.41	15.89	58	49.34	19.32	48	40.69	18.79
388	48.32	16.99	378	44.97	26.18	378	42.62	24.31	357	38.99	25.22

Table 13 / IPI Mathematics, Grades 4–6, 1970/71:
Correlations, All Subjects

	(2) Sex r	(2) Sex N	(3) SES r	(3) SES N	(4) IQ r	(4) IQ N	(5) CTBS concepts r	(5) CTBS concepts N	(6) CTBS problems r	(6) CTBS problems N	(7) CTBS total r	(7) CTBS total N	(8) CRM pretest r	(8) CRM pretest N	(9) CRM posttest r	(9) CRM posttest N	(10) CRM gain r	(10) CRM gain N
(1) Grade	−.05	392	−.03	377	.04	375	.23	378	.19	378	.01	357	.37	388	.32	388	.11	388
(2) Sex			.02	377	−.12	375	−.04	378	−.02	378	−.04	357	.09	388	.08	388	.03	388
(3) SES					.30	364	.16	367	.15	367	.21	347	.07	373	.13	373	.18	373
(4) IQ							.65	366	.56	366	.68	346	.41	372	.43	372	.29	372
(5) CTBS concepts									.67	378	.86	357	.41	374	.44	374	.32	374
(6) CTBS problems											.83	357	.42	374	.44	374	.30	374
(7) CTBS total													.30	353	.38	353	.36	353
(8) CRM pretest															.91	388	.41	388
(9) CRM posttest																	.75	388

Table 14 / IPI Mathematics:
Number of Students in Project Schools in the IPI Curriculum at End of the
1970/71 School Year, by Level

	Level													
	A		B		C		D		E		F		G	
	N	%	N	%	N	%	N	%	N	%	N	%	N	%
Grade 4	2	—	109	8	497	34	777	54	56	4	7	—	0	—
Grade 5	0	—	43	2	291	15	1144	59	400	21	51	3	3	—
Grade 6	0	—	4	—	53	3	545	36	632	41	266	17	33	2

Table 15 / IPI Mathematics:
Number of Students in Alberta Schools in the IPI Curriculum at End of the
1969/70 School Year, by Level

	Level													
	B		C		D		E		F		G		H	
	N	%	N	%	N	%	N	%	N	%	N	%	N	%
Grade 3	2	1	31	19	117	66[a]	25	14[a]	0	—	0	—	0	—
Grade 4	0	—	0	—	51	37	81	59	6	4	0	—	0	—
Grade 5	0	—	0	—	8	7	81	73	21	19	1	1	0	—
Grade 6	0	—	0	—	1	1	33	33	53	53	13	13	1	1

Source: Data from F. D. Oliva, T. O. Maguire, & R. J. Pacey, *IPI project report* (Edmonton: Alberta Human Resources Council, 1971).

[a] Percentages given in the original publication (71 and 7, respectively) have been corrected.

Table 16 / IPI Mathematics:
Number of Students in Oakleaf School in the IPI Curriculum at End of the 1967/68 School Year, by Level

	\multicolumn{2}{c}{B}	\multicolumn{2}{c}{C}	\multicolumn{2}{c}{D}	\multicolumn{2}{c}{E}	\multicolumn{2}{c}{F}	\multicolumn{2}{c}{G}	\multicolumn{2}{c}{H}
	N	%	N	%	N	%	N	%	N	%	N	%	N	%
Grade 3	0	—	1	3	19	59	12	38	0	—	0	—	0	—
Grade 4	0	—	0	—	15	41	16	43	6	16	0	—	0	—
Grade 5	0	—	0	—	5	12	25	58	12	28	1	2	0	—
Grade 6	0	—	0	—	0	—	9	31	13	45	6	21	1	3

Source: Data from R. G. Scanlon, J. Weinberger, & J. Weiler, "IPI as a functioning model for the individualization of instruction," in C. M. Lindvall & R. C. Cox, *Evaluation as a tool in curriculum development: The IPI evaluation program* (Chicago: Rand McNally, 1970), Appendix A.

Table 17 / IPI Mathematics:
Percentage of Grade 5 Pupils Involved in Major Categories of Classroom Activities in an IPI School

Major categories of activity	Mean percentage of pupils engaged in activity	
	Field lab school	Adopting school [a]
Independent work	61.05	41.66
Teacher–pupil activity	7.73	11.84
Noninstructional activity	29.49	41.66
Pupil–pupil activity	1.74	0.22
Group activity	—	—

Source: Data from J. L. Yeager & C. M. Lindvall, "Evaluating an instructional innovation through the observation of pupil activities," *The High School Journal* (1968), **51**, 248-53.

[a] Percentages are as reported in the original text. The failure to add to 100% is no doubt due to the difficulty in recording all children on each round.

Table 18 / IPI Mathematics, 1970/71:
Percentage of Pupil Time Observed in Prespecified Activities

	Mean percentage of time [a]			
Categories of pupil activity	School B	School E	Grand mean	Corrected grand mean [b]
Independent work				
Reading	1.31	2.78	2.04	1.82
Works on worksheet	7.44	0.55	3.99	3.57
Listens individually to tape recorder	0.30	—	0.15	0.13
Views filmstrips				
Checks own work	—	.01	0.00	0.00
Works with language master				
Works with disc-phonograph				
Uses programmed materials	29.55	28.27	28.91	25.87
Corrects a test	0.50	0.23	0.36	0.31
Takes an individual test	14.01	11.84	12.92	12.27
Corrects a study exercise	0.42	0.61	0.51	0.45
Uses supplemental reading material	5.57	8.61	7.09	6.35
Miscellaneous	0.08	12.39	6.23	5.58
Subtotal	59.18	65.29	62.20	55.66
Teacher–pupil activity				
Seeks teacher assistance	0.59	0.89	0.74	0.59
Receives teacher assistance	3.66	1.76	2.71	2.42
Discusses progress with teacher	0.58	1.46	1.02	0.91
Subtotal	4.83	4.11	4.47	4.00
Noninstructional activity				
At desk not working	2.62	1.71	2.16	1.93
Waits for lesson materials				
Waits for prescription	12.94	10.72	11.83	10.59
Goes to get materials	0.02	0.65	0.33	0.30
Waits for papers to be corrected	28.70	20.63	24.66	22.07
Talks to other pupils	1.66	2.68	2.17	1.94
Leaves room to get materials	2.67	0.68	1.67	1.49
Miscellaneous	0.23	4.13	2.18	1.95
Subtotal	48.84	41.20	45.02	40.29

continued

Table 18 – *continued*

	Mean percentage of time [a]			
Categories of pupil activity	School B	School E	Grand mean	Corrected grand mean [b]
Pupil–pupil activity				
Seeks help from other pupil	0.23	0.16	0.20	0.18
Receives help from other pupil	0.10	1.70	0.90	0.81
Subtotal	0.33	1.86	1.09	0.96
Group activity				
Contributes to group discussion				
Takes group test with supervision				
Answers questions				
Asks a question				
Listens to teacher				
Watches film with group				
Listens to records with group				
Watches performance				
Miscellaneous				
Subtotal				
Total [c]	112.85	110.60	111.69	99.96

[a] Percentages are based on means of three observations of each of seven classes at School E and six classes at School B.

[b] Recorded estimates of pupil activity were corrected by computing a weighting factor (0.895).

[c] Necessitated by raters' observation that some pupils were involved in more than one activity during the two-minute observation interval. This accounts for percentages of time exceeding 100%.

References

Abbott, M. Hierarchical impediments to innovation in educational organizations. In M. Abbott and J. Lowell (Eds.), *Change perspectives in educational administration.* Auburn, Ala.: The School of Education, Auburn University, 1965. Pp. 40–53.

Ammerman, H. L. Some important ways in which performance objectives can vary. In W. H. Melching (Ed.), *Deriving, specifying, and using instructional objectives.* Washington, D.C.: Human Resources Research Office, George Washington University, 1966.

Anastasi, A. *Psychological testing.* (2nd ed.) New York: Macmillan, 1961.

Ausubel, D. P. *The psychology of meaningful verbal learning: An introduction to school learning.* New York: Grune & Stratton, 1963.

Bell, G. Formality versus flexibility in complex organizations. In G. Bell (Ed.), *Organizations and human behavior: A book of readings.* Englewood Cliffs, N.J.: Prentice-Hall, 1967. Pp. 97–106.

Benson, D. C., Roberts, W. G., Hedges, H. G., McCallum, Sister Mary Aletha, & Baxter, P. POISE, Phase one. Paper distributed by the Office of Development, The Ontario Institute for Studies in Education, 1969.

Bereiter, C. Education and the pursuit of reality. *Interchange*, 1971, **2**(1), 44–50.

Bialek, H. M., & Castro, B. A second year evaluation of Individually Prescribed Instruction (IPI). Monterey, Calif., November 1968. Cited in *A progress report: Individually Prescribed Instruction.* Philadelphia: Research for Better Schools, 1969.

Blishen, B. R. A socio-economic index for occupations in Canada. *Canadian Review of Sociology and Anthropology*, 1967, **4**(1), 41–53.

Brickell, H. M. *Organizing New York State for educational change.* Albany, N.Y.: State Education Department, 1961.

Brison, D. W., Hedges, H. G., & Robinson, F. G. The use of voluntary aides in the elementary school program: A survey of current practice in the Niagara Region and an analysis of instructional roles. Unpublished manuscript, Niagara Centre (OISE), St. Catharines, 1970.

Brydges, G. An exploration of the effects of anxiety and intelligence on the mathematics performance of elementary school children. Unpublished manuscript, Trent Valley Centre (OISE), Peterborough.

Campbell, D. T., & Stanley, J. C. Experimental and quasi-experimental designs for research on teaching. In N. L. Gage (Ed.), *Handbook of research on teaching: A project of the American Research Association.* Chicago: Rand McNally, 1963.

Carlson, R. O. *Adoption of educational innovations.* Eugene: The Center for the Advanced Study of Educational Administration, University of Oregon, 1965.

Cartier, F. A. Criterion-referenced testing of language skills. *Tesol Quarterly*, 1968, **2**(1), 27–32.

Committee on the Implementation of Change in the Classroom. *Planning and implementing change in Ontario schools: A report on the implementation of change in the classroom.* Toronto: Office of Development, The Ontario Institute for Studies in Education, 1967.

Cox, R. C. Item selection techniques and evaluation of instructional objectives. *Journal of Educational Measurement*, 1965, **2**, 181–85.

Cox, R. C. Evaluative aspects of criterion-referenced measures. Paper presented at the annual meeting of the American Educational Research Association, Minneapolis, March 1970.

Cox, R. C., et al. A description and interim evaluation report concerning the first two years of the Individually Prescribed Instruction project. Learning Research and Development Center, University of Pittsburgh, December 1966. Cited in *A progress report: Individually Prescribed Instruction*. Philadelphia: Research for Better Schools, 1969.

Cox, R. C., & Graham, G. T. The development of a sequentially scaled achievement test. *Journal of Educational Measurement*, 1966, **3**(2), 147–50.

Cox, R. C., & Vargas, J. S. A comparison of item selection techniques for norm-referenced and criterion-referenced tests. Paper presented at the annual meeting of the National Council on Measurement in Education, Chicago, 1966.

Cronbach, L. J. Course improvement through evaluation. *Teachers College Record*, 1963, **64**(8), 672–83.

Denison, E. F. The sources of economic growth in the United States and the alternatives before us. Supplementary Paper No. 13, Committee for Economic Development, 1962.

Denison, E. F. Appendix to Edward F. Denison's reply. In Study Group in the Economics of Education, *The residual factor and economic growth.* Paris: Organization for Economic Co-operation and Development, 1964. Pp. 86–100.

Dewey, J. *Democracy and education: An introduction to the philosophy of education.* New York: Macmillan, 1916. (Republished: New York, The Free Press, 1966.)

Dressel, P. L. Measurement and evaluation. In *Thirteenth Yearbook, American Association of Colleges for Teacher Education*, 1960. Pp. 45–52.

Ebel, R. L. Some comments by Robert L. Ebel. *The School Review*, 1967 (Winter), 261–66.

Eisner, E. W. Education objectives: Help or hindrance? *The School Review*, 1967 (Winter), 250–82.

Estes, N. Issues in implementation. Paper presented at the third Conference on Education Accountability, sponsored by the Educational Testing Service, Princeton, N.J., June 1971. (Tape available.)

Evans, J., McIntyre, E., Pohland, P., Rigsby, L., Russell, H. H., & Smith, L. *Evaluation of computer assisted instruction.* St. Anne, Mo.: Central Midwestern Regional Educational Laboratory, 1969.

Ferguson, G. A. *Statistical analysis in psychology and education.* New York: McGraw-Hill, 1959.

Fisher, J. R. An investigation of three approaches to the teaching of mathematics in the elementary school. Unpublished doctoral dissertation, University of Pittsburgh, 1967.

Forehand, G. A. The role of the evaluator in curriculum research. *Journal of Educational Measurement*, 1966, **3**(3), 199–204.

Fullan, M., & Eastabrook, G. Problems and issues in defining school innovativeness. Paper presented at the annual meeting of the Ontario Educational Research Council, Toronto, 1970.

Fullan, M., Eastabrook, G., & Hewson, P. A new look at school innovativeness. Paper presented at the annual meeting of the Canadian Sociology and Anthropology Association, St. John's, Nfld., 1971.

Gagné, R. M. *The conditions of learning.* New York: Holt, Rinehart & Winston, 1965.

Galbraith, J. K. *The affluent society.* Boston: Houghton-Mifflin, 1958.

Gallagher, P. K. The evaluation of student achievement in the individually prescribed program in mathematics at the Frank A. Berry School, Bethel, Conn. Graduate School of Education, Fairfield University, May 1968. Cited in *A progress report: Individually Prescribed Instruction.* Philadelphia: Research for Better Schools, 1969.

Garvin, A. D. The applicability of criterion-referenced measurement by content area and level. Paper presented at the joint annual meeting of the American Educational Research Association and National Council on Measurement in Education, Minneapolis, March 1970.

Glaser, R. Instructional technology and the measurement of learning outcomes: Some questions. *American Psychologist*, 1963, **18**, 519–21.

Glaser, R. Evaluation of instruction and changing educational models. From the Proceedings of the Symposium on Problems in the Evaluation of Instruction, University of California, Los Angeles, December 1967.

Glaser, R., & Cox, R. C. Criterion-referenced testing for the measurement of educational outcomes. In R. A. Weisberger (Ed.), *Instructional process and media innovation.* Chicago: Rand McNally, 1968. Pp. 545–50.

Goslin, D. A. *The school in contemporary society.* New York: Scott, Foresman, 1963.

Gottlieb, D., & Brookover, W. B. *Acceptance of new educational practices by elementary school teachers.* East Lansing, Mich.: Educational Publication Services, College of Education, Michigan State University, 1966.

Guttman, L. A basis for scaling qualitative ideas. *American Sociological Review*, 1944, **9**, 139–50.

Hastings, J. T. Some comments by J. Thomas Hastings. *The School Review*, 1967 (Winter), 167–71.

Hedges, H. G. Volunteer parental assistance in elementary schools. Unpublished doctoral dissertation, The Ontario Institute for Studies in Education, 1972.

Hoke, J. M. Parental opinions of the pilot project in IPI arithmetic. In F. D. Oliva, T. O. Maguire, & R. J. Pacey. *IPI project report*. Edmonton: Alberta Human Resources Research Council, 1971.

Hummel, R. C., & Cox, L. S. Change in teacher attitudes toward decision-making and school organization. Paper presented at the annual meeting of the American Educational Research Association, Minneapolis, March 1970.

Ireton, H., Thwing, E., & Gravem, H. Infant mental development and neurological status, family socioeconomic status, and intelligence at age four. *Child Development*, 1970, **41**(4), 937–45.

Jackson, R. *Developing criterion-referenced tests*. Princeton, N.J.: Educational Resources Information Center Clearinghouse on tests, measurement and evaluation, 1970.

King, E. M. *Manual for the Canadian Tests of Basic Skills*. Toronto: Thomas Nelson & Sons, 1967.

Kivlin, J. E. Characteristics of farm practices associated with rate of adoption. Doctoral dissertation, Pennsylvania State University, 1960. Cited in E. M. Rogers, *Diffusion of innovations*. New York: Free Press of Glencoe, 1962.

Leithwood, K. A. Evaluating achievement of educational objectives. *Orbit*, 1971, **2**(4), 10–11.

Lindvall, C. M., & Bolvin, J. O. The role of the teacher in Individually Prescribed Instruction. *Educational Technology*, 1970, **10**(2), 37–41.

Lindvall, C. M., & Nitko, A. J. *Criterion-referenced testing and the individualization of instruction*. Philadelphia: Research for Better Schools, 1969.

Lippitt, R., et al. The teacher as innovator, seeker and sharer of new practices. In R. Miller (Ed.), *Perspectives on educational change*. New York: Appleton-Century-Crofts, 1967. Pp. 307–24.

Living and learning: The report of the Provincial Committee on Aims and Objectives of Education in the Schools of Ontario. Toronto: The Ontario Department of Education, 1968.

Madaus, G. F., & Airasian, P. W. Placement, formative, diagnostic and summative evaluation of classroom learning. Paper presented at the annual meeting of the American Educational Research Association, Minneapolis, March 1970.

Mager, R. F. *Preparing instructional objectives*. Palo Alto, Calif.: Fearon Publishers, 1962.

McGill, S., & Skinner, G. The effect of an experimental program on classroom behavior in elementary school. Unpublished manuscript, Trent Valley Centre (OISE), Peterborough, 1970.

Mehlinger, H. D., & Patrick, J. J. The use of "formative" and "summative" evaluation in an experimental curriculum project: A case in the practice of instructional materials evaluation. Paper presented at the annual meeting of the American Educational Research Association, Minneapolis, March 1970.

Melching, W. H. (Ed.). *Deriving, specifying and using instructional objectives*. Washington, D.C.: Human Resources Research Office, George Washington University, 1966.

Miles, M. B. (Ed.). *Innovations in education.* New York: Teachers College Press, Columbia University, 1964.

Miles, M. Education and innovation: The organization as context. In M. Abbott & J. Lowell (Eds.), *Change perspectives in educational administration.* Auburn, Ala.: The School of Education, Auburn University, 1965. Pp. 54–72.

Miller, G. A., Galanter, E. N., & Pribram, K. H. *Plans and the structure of behavior.* New York: Holt, Rinehart & Winston, 1960.

Millman, J. Reporting student progress: A case for a criterion-referenced marking system. *Evaluation and Measurement Newsletter* (OISE), 1971, no. 10.

Montgomery, R. D. An evaluation of the POISE program at Queen Mary School. Unpublished manuscript, Trent Valley Centre (OISE), Peterborough, 1970.

Oliva, F. D., Maguire, T. O., & Pacey, R. J. *IPI project report.* Edmonton: Alberta Human Resources Research Council, 1971.

Popham, W. J. Probing the validity of arguments against behavioral goals. Paper presented at the annual meeting of the American Educational Research Association, Chicago, March 1968.

Popham, W. J. The instructional objectives exchange: New support for criterion-referenced instruction. *Evaluation and Measurement Newsletter* (OISE), 1971, no. 10.

Popham, W. J., & Husek, T. R. Implications of criterion-referenced measurement. *Journal of Educational Measurement,* 1969, **6**, 1–9.

Pratt, D. Nine criteria for educational objectives. Paper presented at the annual meeting of the Canadian Association of Professors of Education, St. John's, Nfld., 1971.

Provus, M. Evaluation of ongoing programs in the public school system. In *Yearbook of the National Society for the Study of Education.* Chicago: National Society for the Study of Education, 1969. Pp. 242–83.

Regan, E. M. The Conceptual Skills Program – a "thinking" program for kindergarten children. *Orbit,* 1970, **1**(4), 16–18.

Research for Better Schools, Inc. *IPI evaluation summary, 1967–68: Status report.* Philadelphia: Research for Better Schools, 1968.

Research for Better Schools, Inc. *A progress report: Individually Prescribed Instruction.* Philadelphia: Research for Better Schools, 1969.

Research for Better Schools, Inc., and Learning Research and Development Center, University of Pittsburgh. Summary of a conference of teachers and administrators using the instructional system Individually Prescribed Instruction. February 1967.

Rigsby, L., & McIntyre, E. In J. Evans, E. McIntyre, P. Pohland, L. Rigsby, H. H. Russell, & L. Smith *Evaluation of Computer Assisted Instruction.* St. Anne, Mo.: Central Midwestern Regional Educational Laboratory, 1969.

Rogers, E. M. *Diffusion of innovations.* New York: Free Press of Glencoe, 1962.

Scanlon, R. G., Weinberger, J., & Weiler, J. IPI as a functioning model for the individualization of instruction. In C. M. Lindvall & R. C. Cox, *Evaluation as a tool in curriculum development: The IPI evaluation program.* Chicago: Rand McNally, 1970. Appendix A.

Scardemalia, M., & Bereiter, C. *A field test of the Conceptual Skills Program.* Toronto: The Ontario Institute for Studies in Education, 1971.

Scriven, M. The methodology of evaluation. In R. W. Tyler, R. M. Gagné, & M. Scriven, *Perspectives of curriculum evaluation*. Chicago: Rand McNally, 1967. Pp. 39–83.

Senathirajah, N., & Weiss, J. *Evaluation in geography: A resource book for teachers*. Toronto: The Ontario Institute for Studies in Education, 1971.

Shoemaker, D. M. Evaluating the effectiveness of competing instructional programs. *Educational Researcher*, 1972, **1**(5), 5–12.

Stake, R. E. Toward a technology for the evaluation of educational programs. In R. W. Tyler, R. M. Gagné, & M. Scriven, *Perspectives of curriculum evaluation*. Chicago: Rand McNally, 1967. Pp. 1–12.

Stake, R. E. Generalizability of program evaluation: The need for limits. *Educational Product Report*, 1969, **2** (February), 39–40.

Stake, R. E. Focus on portrayal. *Evaluation and Measurement Newsletter* (OISE), 1972, no. 14.

Stake, R. E., & Denny, T. Needed concepts and techniques for utilizing more fully the potential of evaluation. In *Yearbook of the National Society for the Study of Education*. Chicago: National Society for the Study of Education, 1969. Pp. 370–90.

Tyler, R. W. The objectives and plans for a national assessment of educational progress. *Journal of Educational Measurement*, 1966, **3**(1), 1–4.

Unfinished business in the teaching profession. *Phi Delta Kappan*, 1970, **52**(1).

Ward, J. On the concept of criterion-referenced measurement. *British Journal of Educational Psychology*, 1970, **40**, 314–23.

Watson, G. Toward a conceptual architecture of self-renewing school system. In G. Watson (Ed.), *Change in school systems*. Washington, D.C.: National Training Laboratories, National Education Association, 1967.

Weiss, J. Formative curriculum evaluation: In need of methodology. Paper presented at the annual meeting of the American Educational Research Association, New York, 1971.

Whitehead, A. N. *The aims of education*. New York: Macmillan, 1956.

Yeager, J. L., & Lindvall, C. M. Evaluating an instructional innovation through the observation of pupil activities. *The High School Journal*, 1968, **51**, 248–53.

Other OISE Publications on the Subject of Innovation

Volunteer Helpers in Elementary Schools
Floyd Robinson, David Brison, Henry Hedges, Jane Hill, and Cecilia Yau
A systematic study of the use of volunteers for both teaching and non-teaching functions in school programs in the Niagara region of Ontario. Includes case studies and information on how to conduct a similar survey.   33 pages, 1971.

The York County Board of Education:
A Study in Innovation
Jan J. Loubser, Herbert Spiers, and Carolyn Moody
A short study exploring the way in which the York County Board of Education implements and evaluates innovation showing how the flexible structure of its educational system is conducive to innovation. Three specific innovative practices are studied: the curriculum committee, the master-teacher program, and the organization development unit.   54 pages, 1972.

Thornlea:
A Case Study of an Innovative Secondary School
Michael Fullan, Glenn Eastabrook, Dan Spinner, and Jan J. Loubser
A description of the goals of Thornlea Secondary School, its administrative and social structure, and the process used to implement innovations. Examines a number of specific innovations, giving particular attention to the "Community and I" course and the instructional policy committee.   46 pages, 1972.

The School in Transition:
A Profile of a Secondary School Undergoing Innovation
Alan J. C. King and Reginald Ripton
Describes and considers the implications of two forms of secondary school organization – a traditional system and an innovative system incorporating individual timetables, a credit system, subject promotion, and a student-centered approach to discipline. A joint project of OISE and the Ottawa Board of Education.
52 pages, 1970.

Innovative Secondary Schools
Alan J. C. King
A continuation of the study of innovative secondary schools reported in *The School*

in Transition examining three innovative secondary schools and one traditional school and focusing on the changes innovation implies for administrators, teachers, and students. Outlines problems resulting from the switch to individual timetabling and the credit system, and suggests to schools in the process of change how to gain the most benefit from the system. A joint project of the Ottawa Board of Education and the Faculty of Education, Queen's University.   58 pages, 1972.

Prices and topics of the catalogue listing these and other OISE publications may be obtained from Publications Sales, The Ontario Institute for Studies in Education, 252 Bloor Street West, Toronto, Ontario M5S 1V6.